*Andrew Johnson*

ENGRAVED AND PRINTED
AT THE
BUREAU OF ENGRAVING & PRINTING,
U.S.
TREASURY DEPARTMENT.

# MEMORIAL ADDRESSES

ON THE

## LIFE AND CHARACTER

OF

# ANDREW JOHNSON,

(A SENATOR FROM TENNESSEE,)

DELIVERED IN THE

## SENATE AND HOUSE OF REPRESENTATIVES,

JANUARY 12, 1876.

PUBLISHED BY ORDER OF CONGRESS.

FORTY-FOURTH CONGRESS, FIRST SESSION.

1876.

PROCEEDINGS

IN THE

SENATE OF THE UNITED STATES.

# ADDRESSES.

### ADDRESS OF MR. COOPER, OF TENNESSEE.

Mr. President, upon me devolves the sad duty of formally announcing to the Senate the death of Hon. ANDREW JOHNSON, late a Senator from the State of Tennessee.

On the 31st day of July, 1875, near his mountain home in East Tennessee, surrounded by family and friends, he passed from earth to meet his reward. The event was a shock to the people of the State who had so recently honored him by an election through their representatives to a seat in this body; it was a shock to the nation, whose highest offices he had filled.

The conflicts of party in which he freely mingled are too recent not to have left deep scars; but throughout our mighty Republic everywhere there were those who delighted to do him honor. The greater part of his life was passed in the public service; much of that time in the councils of the nation; and having almost reached his three-score years and ten, the scriptural limit of human life, he has passed the portals of the tomb, been claimed by the insatiate archer, his spirit summoned to God who gave it, and his body consigned to the place appointed for the dead.

He will no more go in and out before us. No more will his voice be heard in this Chamber. No more will expectant friends crowd these galleries, to hang upon his words and catch the inspiration which he was accustomed to impart to them by the fervor of his utterances. Nor will the Senate again be edified or instructed by his exposition of the Constitution, or the enunciation of his opinions, lucid and mature as they always were. Life is ended. The mortal has put on immortality, and what he has accomplished for the good of mankind alone remains to us of this tribune of the people.

Senators, how frequent of late have been these visits of death to this Chamber! Since our separation in March last, once and again, and yet again, has he accomplished his mission, and three of our associates been called from our assemblies here to meet the realities of the future and eternal life. The genial smile and friendly greeting of our honored and revered friend, the late Vice-President, will no more be seen and felt by us. His generous heart has ceased to be affected by earthly woes.

Nor shall we again be permitted to listen to the words of wisdom and instruction with which the late Senator from Connecticut [Mr. FERRY] was accustomed to edify and enlighten the Senate. He, too, has been called to a higher sphere and a nobler work. Well may we exclaim, in the language of the righteous man of Uz, "Have pity upon me, O ye my friends; for the hand of God hath touched me."

Few men have been more prominent or commanded to a greater extent the attention of the people than Mr. Johnson.

After his entrance upon public life his career was marked by warm friendships and fierce antagonisms. He courted controversy and shrank not when the contest came. In this and the other House he was reckoned among those who contended for the mastery. He was often in the fiercest of the conflict, and was not wanting in success. During his terms of service he participated in most of the debates which took place upon the questions then agitated in Congress. He also engaged as a public speaker before the people in all the canvasses which were waged after he became a public man. Few speakers excelled him in depth of conviction or in earnestness of utterance. He exercised in an eminent degree the faculty of attracting the attention of his hearers and retaining it with unflagging interest to the end. Many of his speeches have been preserved, but will fail to give to those who may read them in the future an adequate idea of their power upon those who heard them.

His state papers while President will be the most lasting monument of his claim to greatness as a statesman. Many of them are productions which have seldom, if ever, been excelled.

But this is neither a suitable nor proper occasion to pass them in review, or to discuss their merits, or to compare them with the productions of others, or to speak of the principles advocated. All this belongs to those who may come after us, to those who will write history, and who will assign each contestant for the world's honor his proper niche in the temple of fame.

Mr. JOHNSON was conspicuous in every position in which he was placed. Whether in the halls of legislation or in the executive departments of government he commanded attention. Whether as governor, directing the affairs of a single State, or in the presidential chair, superintending the affairs of this great nation, the mass of his countrymen award him the highest praise, and insist that his conduct will bear favorable comparison with the purest and best of those who preceded him in office.

His aim in the discharge of the high duties devolving upon him in his exalted office, so far as we can know it from official action, was to know the Constitution and to follow it. A firm believer himself in the capacity of man for self-government, and that our form of government furnished the best model that has ever been devised for proving the truth of the theory, he sought earnestly to carry into practice its every precept. In his opinion the people may always be trusted to do right. They will never do wrong intentionally. And if they do err, it will be through the influence of trusted leaders, and but momentarily; "their second sober thought" will always bring them back to the path of safety, rectitude, and progress. To them he confidently looked for the remedy of any fault which might be developed in the working of our system of government. He trusted the people implicitly, and never doubted that they would see and prevent any subversion of their liberties or restraint of their rights and privileges.

He was indeed a tribune of the people. In his care their dearest rights and interests were secure, so far as intentional injury upon his part was concerned. He was one of the people, felt for them, sympathized with them, and, they believed, was ready to do all in his power for their political advancement. Hence the devotion of the masses for him. The theater of his power and greatness was before the masses. He swayed them by the earnestness of his eloquence and the conviction which he aroused in them of the sincerity of his beliefs and purposes. Few men have shown greater power in arousing the people and attaching them to his fortunes than did Mr. JOHNSON. The secret lay in his own firm convictions and his unwavering belief in the patriotism, good sense, and integrity of the masses, that they desired to do right and would do so in the end, together with the faculty, which he possessed in an eminent degree, of impressing the truthfulness of these convictions upon his hearers. But why should I dwell upon that which is so familiar to all who knew him; and who is there to whom he was unknown?

His public life is known to all the people. The most trying scenes in it are of too recent occurrence and too important in their effects upon the nation to be easily forgotten. I will not enter upon the vain task of attempting to add anything to his fame. In this place, where he was so well known, amid those many of whom were actors in the most important event of his eventful life, why portray the past? Why dwell upon his merit, which will now be so readily admitted?

But he will no more be seen among us. He has been called to meet the Judge of all the earth. The places which knew him here will know him no more forever. Another has been called to fill his vacant chair and charged with the performance of the duties which so recently devolved upon him. "Alas, how soon we are forgotten," is a truth felt by all who have lived to man's estate. Yet there are some the memory of whose deeds will long survive and whose names the world will not willingly forget. May we not hope that our lamented colleague will be one in this roll of honor? Death has purified his fame. His faults will be forgotten and his virtues cherished. In this spirit I lay my wreath upon his tomb.

Mr. President, I offer for present consideration the following resolutions:

*Resolved,* That the Senate has received with profound sorrow the announcement of the death of Hon. ANDREW JOHNSON, late a Senator of the United States from the State of Tennessee.

*Resolved,* That as a mark of respect for the memory of Mr. JOHNSON, the members of the Senate will go into mourning by wearing crape upon the left arm for thirty days.

*Resolved,* That, as an additional mark of respect for the memory of Mr. JOHNSON, the Senate do now adjourn.

*Ordered,* That the Secretary communicate these resolutions to the House of Representatives.

ADDRESS OF MR. MORTON, OF INDIANA.

Mr. President, as a member of this body, in the discharge of what I regarded as a high official duty, I voted for the impeachment of ANDREW JOHNSON. I believed he had violated the law; and for that vote I have no excuse or apology to offer; but, sir, I would let the memory of what I regarded as his faults be buried with him, and choose to remember only his virtues and his services to his country. I would exercise for him the same charity that I would ask to have extended to myself in the inevitable hour.

Mr. JOHNSON was a man of remarkable traits of character. He was distinguished for his tenacity of purpose, perhaps for his impatience of opposition. He was combative in his temperament; and that quality of his mind, I have no doubt, led him to do many of those things to which objection was taken. He was born in the humble walks of life; he lived in poverty, and had no advantages of early education. I have heard it said that his wife taught him to read. But he was distinguished for his thirst for knowledge and for an honorable ambition, and he went up step by step; first, holding an office in the town in which he lived, and afterward in the Legislature of Tennessee; then a member of the other House of Congress, and then a member of this body. In every position in life he showed himself to be a man of ability and of courage, and I believe it is proper to say of Andrew Johnson that his honesty has never been suspected; the smell of corruption was never upon his garments.

As a member of this body, in 1858, he introduced a bill granting a homestead of one hundred and sixty acres of land to every actual settler. He was far in advance of the statesmen of his own section, and even those of the North, upon that question. It was a measure that was not popular in the South, for reasons which we can all understand, but which it is not necessary to advert to now. That measure did not become a law then, though it did afterward; but Mr. Johnson was entitled to none the less credit for his early and bold advocacy of it. The establishment of the homestead was almost an era in the history of this country. It was one of the greatest blessings that was ever conferred by a single act of Congress.

When the storm of secession swept over the South and through this Hall, Andrew Johnson was the only member of Congress from the South in either House, so far as I remember, who resisted that wave and stood faithfully to the Union. In introducing this matter, of course I desire to arouse no partisan feeling here, but simply to do justice to his history. It cost something to be a Union man in the South. These Southern Senators can testify to that. It required courage and daring that were not required to take a similar position in the North. Mr.

Johnson understood full well that it would cost him the friendship of his life-long neighbors in Tennessee; that it would, at least for a time, make him an outcast from their society; that he might even become an exile from the State in which he had lived and which he had so long and so ably served; but he stood in this Chamber and declared his devotion to the Union, turned his back upon those seductive influences to go with the South in that terrible controversy, defied their threats, hurled back with indignation the epithets that had been launched upon him. He made a speech here on the 5th and 6th days of February, 1861, which I have taken the pains to hunt up. I remember the effect of those words as they rang through the North. In the course of that speech Mr. Johnson said:

> Sir, I intend to stand by that flag, and by the Union of which it is the emblem. I agree with Mr. A. H. Stephens, of Georgia, "that this Government of our fathers, with all its defects, comes nearer the objects of all good governments than any other on the face of the earth."

And again he said:

> I have been told, and I have heard it repeated, that this Union is gone. It has been said in this Chamber that it is in the cold sweat of death; that, in fact, it is really dead, and merely lying in state waiting for the funeral obsequies to be performed. If this be so, and the war that has been made upon me in consequence of advocating the Constitution and the Union is to result in my overthrow and in my destruction, and that flag, that glorious flag, the emblem of the Union, which was borne by Washington through a seven years' struggle, shall be struck from the Capitol and trailed in the dust; when this Union is interred, I want no more honorable winding-sheet than that brave old flag, and no more glorious grave than to be interred in the tomb of the Union.

Those were brave words to be uttered by Andrew Johnson under the circumstances. I admired and honored him at the time; I do so now, and ever shall. He was a brave man, and he encountered risks and subjected himself to dangers which we of the North scarcely knew anything about. Perhaps no man in Congress exerted the same influence on the public sentiment of the North at the beginning of the war as ANDREW JOHNSON.

Afterward, in the spring of 1862, I think it was in March, Mr. Lincoln appointed him military governor of the State of Tennessee. He went there at the imminent risk of his life. He was subjected to violence, I think at Lynchburgh, on the road; and when he arrived at Nashville he was threatened with assassination on the streets and in public assemblies; but he went on the streets; he defied those dangers; he went into public assemblies, and on one occasion went into a public meeting, drew his pistol, laid it on the desk before him, and said, "I have been told that I should be assassinated if I came here. If that is to be done, then it is the first business in order, and let that be attended to." No attempt having been made, he said: "I conclude the danger has passed by;" and then he proceeded to make his speech. His conduct as military governor was distinguished for courage, for devotion to the interests of the Union; and the admiration created by his conduct throughout the North led to his nomination for Vice-President upon the republican ticket in 1864. He was elected, and afterward became President of the United States by the assassination of Mr. Lincoln.

We were personal friends. The first time I ever met Mr. JOHNSON was in this Chamber. I was on a casual visit here, and heard the debate in which Mr. Breckinridge made his final speech before leaving to join the confederate army. I was introduced to Mr. JOHNSON then, and from that time we were friends. After I had voted for his impeachment, and met him accidentally, he wore the same kindly smile as in times before, and offered me his hand. I thought it showed nobility of soul. There were not many men who could have done that.

He has gone! We are all soon to follow him. If he had his faults, let them be buried with him. Let us remember the great services he rendered to his country. He was faithful to his country in a time of great trial, and let that fidelity and those great services always be remembered.

ADDRESS OF MR. McCREERY, OF KENTUCKY.

Mr. President, the Senator of Indiana [Mr. Morton] introduced his remarks by a reference to the impeachment trial. I will say that I had the honor to be one of the Senators who voted for acquittal on that occasion. Like him, I have no apologies to make for that vote.

Death has stricken a great name from the roll of the Senate. The providence of God is over us, and we bow reverently to the dispensation, even though the bonds of brotherhood are broken. The mortal remains of Andrew Johnson lie buried under the soil of Tennessee. His record as a statesman is finished. His career, with its toils, its struggles, and its anxieties, is completed. We turn for a few moments from the discharge of our ordinary duties to make this last sad offering to the memory of that extraordinary man, and his name and his fame are ready for history. He was plain and simple in his manners and tastes, and if it were possible for him to exert a controlling influence over the solemn exercises of this hour, he would prefer the words of soberness and truth to the exaggeration and extravagance of eulogy. In the walks of private life he was considered a good citizen. He spoke the truth, paid his taxes, settled his just debts; he was an honest man. So well was he established in that regard, that where he was best known his bitterest enemy would resent even an insinuation that he had been guilty of duplicity, falsehood, or fraud in any of his business transactions. Senator Brownlow has never been conspicuous for moderation in controversy, neither has he been extravagant, but, on the contrary, exceedingly economical and frugal, in the use of compliment toward his adversaries; but that Senator, in the long years of their fierce antagonism, not only never assailed, but he never failed on proper occasion, before or after the death of JOHNSON, to vindicate his integrity. Integrity was the foundation upon which he reared the superstructure of his political fortune. He enjoyed more of the confidence and respect than he did of the personal regard and esteem of his fellow-citizens. He had not the dash which sometimes elevates an empty-headed demagogue to great popularity, which leaves him as suddenly and perhaps as unexpectedly as it was acquired. He wore a sad expression, and his conversation was neither witty nor brilliant, but direct and to the point. If it possessed any charm, it was due in a measure to the modulations of a clear, mellow voice, the tones of which rose and fell as passion, interest, or indifference predominated at the moment. These, however, were not even elements of his strength. The people believed he was honest, they knew he was capable, and that was enough for them.

If the departed Senator belonged to any church, it must have been to the church militant, for life with him was a warfare from beginning to end. He was aggressive, unyielding, uncompromising. When smitten, he forgot the injunction and smote the smiter, and the battle was measured by resource and endurance. Christian or Moslem stood by the symbol of his faith with no more tenacity and resolution than he displayed in defense of his principles. He enjoyed triumph with moderation, but it cannot be said that he bore defeat with true philosophy. If he had reflected that position was as desirable to others as to himself, it might have turned the edge of his resentment. The champion of popular rights had little respect even for a popular verdict adverse to himself, and a new trial and a re-argument of the cause were demanded.

Justice to ANDREW JOHNSON requires at least an allusion to his humble origin, to his early orphanage, and to his poverty at the outset of life. He had learned the trade of a tailor, and the work on the board might be said to constitute the boundary of his useful knowledge. But an angel had taken her place by his side to share his joys and his sorrows, and to cheer and to bless and to enlighten him by her counsel and instruction. He labored diligently for her support, and she more than canceled the obligation by gently dispelling the dark shadows and imparting light and life and energy to his understanding. She prepared him to stand forth in the stature and strength of manhood, and to discharge the highest and most responsible duties of an American citizen. He was not the creature of accident nor the offspring of chance, but a self-reliant man, of steady purpose and iron will, who started from the bottom, and from a village alderman rose rapidly through the different grades of the public service to the most exalted position upon earth. After a few years of private life he was returned by his State to the Senate under circumstances peculiar in some respects. He was the first Ex-President who had entered the Senate, and it was understood that he acknowledged no special fealty and no particular partiality to any political organization. Much was expected from him. Whether the highest hopes and expectations of his friends and admirers would have been realized or not is a matter of conjecture concerning which every man will enjoy his own opinion.

I never heard a speech from him until a short time before our final separation. That speech was published as delivered, without revision or correction. Critics may discover redundancy and repetition, but we who heard it know that it was a powerful appeal in behalf of the Constitution. Other speakers may have been as logical and as eloquent, but no man spoke with more earnestness than he did. He related no anecdotes, and aimed at no pleasantries; but voice, manner, and diction rose to the level of the great question he was considering, and Senate and galleries listened with profound attention. The unvarying earnestness of his delivery may have been the secret of his power and the key to his strong hold upon the confidence of the people of Tennessee. But speculation is idle; we only know that from a most unpromising beginning he accomplished surprising and wonderful results. When he went to Greeneville he was a stranger, and a tailor's "kit," his thimbles and his needles, were probably the sum-total of his earthly possessions; at his death, the hills and the valleys and the mountains and the rivers sent forth their thousands to testify to the general grief at the irreparable loss.

I honor him for that manly courage which sustained him on every occasion, and which never quailed in presence of opposition, no matter how imposing. I honor him for that independence of soul which had no scorn for the lowly and no cringing adulation for the exalted. I honor him for that sterling integrity which was beyond the reach of temptation, and which, at the close of his public service, left no blot, no stain upon his escutcheon. I honor him for that magnanimity which, after the war-cloud had passed and the elements had settled, would have brought every citizen under the radiant arch of the bow of peace and pardon.

It is the province of patriotism to guard the ashes and to cherish and perpetuate the memories of the mighty dead. Every locality has its particular treasures. Jackson, Polk, and JOHNSON! Will these names be forgotten in Tennessee? The sun and the stars will shine in their seasons, but revolving years will neither quench nor dim the light of their great examples.

Address of Mr. Merrimon, of North Carolina.

Mr. President, it seems to me appropriate that the voice of North Carolina should join in these solemn ceremonies. There our late associate, the late Ex-President Johnson, was born, and there he began his remarkable career which rendered him famous in this and other lands. The people of that State watched with more than ordinary interest his eventful life—sometimes approvingly and at others with disapprobation; they recognized his marked ability, his industry and self-reliance, his courage and fortitude, his firmness and integrity, his successes and his triumphs; they condemned his faults, but over them they have cast the mantle of charity and forgetfulness, and they have shared largely and sincerely in the general sorrow occasioned by his sudden death.

My personal acquaintance with Mr. Johnson began shortly after I became a member of the Senate; it was brief and agreeable, and served to strengthen my impressions of his character derived from a general knowledge of him for a long while as a prominent public man. He was not only a distinguished citizen, but in many respects he was one of the great men of his country and of the age in which he lived. His cast of mind, his character, and successes in life present an interesting study in connection with our political institutions and their peculiar workings in the development of the talents and virtues of men in every class and condition of society. He did what few have accomplished in the course of time. From a birth, a boyhood, and circumstances the most humble and untoward, without aid and without extraordinary advantages at any period of his life, often under the frowns of the great and powerful, by the exercise of his own powers and his own efforts, he passed gradually, and always with distinction, through stations small and great until he reached and filled with striking ability, and under circumstances the most trying, one of the most exalted on earth.

Without intending here to approve or disapprove his general course of action, if we consider fairly the extraordinary, perilous, and revolutionary circumstances that surrounded the country at the time he filled the high station of President, it may well be doubted whether any of the great men who at different periods filled that place could have ruled and subdued the storm of passion and partisan fury that threatened to ingulf the Government more successfully than he did. Whatever the unfriendly critic may say, all disinterested men will agree that he filled most of the many stations he occupied with great acceptability and all of them with great credit to himself. I think it may be fairly said of him that in all the responsible places he filled he never failed to prove himself equal to the duties devolved upon him. Doubtless he did not discharge them acceptably to all; but all must admit that he did so with distinguished ability. For his elevation and distinction he was not indebted to any sudden freak of fortune in arms or civil life, but to his native talents, his efforts, and his persistency in sunshine and storm alike. He lacked the polish of high culture and training, but he possessed in a large degree the moral, intellectual, and physical power to command fortune. This epitome of his life marks him one of the strong and great men of his age.

Mr. JOHNSON possessed a strong, logical, and aggressive mind and a powerful will. He had stern integrity, which he carried into all the relations of life; indeed, this was one of his leading and striking characteristics; he was remarkable for his honesty, and—

To be honest, as this world goes, is to be one man picked out of ten thousand.

His moral and physical courage was unbending, often rising to heroism. The adverse circumstances of his early life deprived him of the essential advantages of youthful education and training, but he overleaped this obstacle; he was self-educated; he had not the finish of systematic culture, nor could he claim great learning, but he thought, wrote, and spoke strongly and intelligently on all subjects that engaged his attention. Some of his state papers will compare favorably with the best. He had an extensive and correct knowledge of human nature and large insight into the motives of men. He measured them at a glance mentally and morally, and generally with singular accuracy. He had administrative capacity of no ordinary mold or measure.

He was always thoroughly and honestly in sympathy with the masses of the people and popular government. He was essentially a man of the people; and however he may sometimes have erred in judgment looking to that end, he zealously desired their welfare and happiness. He made them believe so, and this may be reckoned one of the strongest elements of his power with, before, and over the masses of his fellow-countrymen.

He made mistakes, some of them grave ones; but who is free from error? He had faults; he may have had serious ones; it were strange indeed if, under the conflicts and temptations of his life, he were free from them. And let me ask, what man of us is free from them? His virtues and pariotism far outweighed and outmeasured his errors and follies. Let us keep fresh in our memory the former, and over the latter let the mantle of charity be cast.

I well remember how on the 4th of March last, when he entered this Chamber to take his seat again as a member of the Senate, his countrymen, crowding the galleries and corridors, saluted him with loud and spontaneous applause, and how they did a second time, when he stepped forward to be sworn. Admiring, tasteful, and delicate friends had richly adorned his desk with beautiful and expressive flowers, and when that day the Senate adjourned hundreds of his friends, and men, too, who had in the past been unfriendly toward him, hurried to his seat to tender him respect and sincere congratulations. That was a grand occasion for him, and his heart was glad!

He was not an aged man. His friends had hoped that he would be spared to his country many years to come to do much and noble service for that country. But his work is done; his labors are ended. Death suddenly snatched him away from the scenes, the conflicts and sorrows, the pleasures and the honors of this life, and he is gone to try the realities of eternal things. May his countrymen remember and emulate his virtues and his noble deeds.

Address of Mr. Paddock, of Nebraska.

Mr. President, it is with no ordinary diffidence that I arise to address the Senate upon an occasion of so much interest as the present. The fear that I, who have so recently come among you, may commit an offense against the proprieties which should be as a law unto us all in this Chamber, almost overwhelms me. Indeed, sir, so much has already been so appropriately, so eloquently said by my seniors here, whose fame is the very fame of the Republic itself, that my poor words, however fitly spoken, will, I doubt not, be considered presumptuous. But, sir, I am impelled by a sense of duty to the State I have the honor to represent, in part, upon this floor, to briefly express, on the behalf of all the people thereof, of whatever party, sect, or class, the universal sorrow occasioned there by the death of Andrew Johnson. Especially, sir, do I offer here for the memory of the departed Senator the gratitude and the unselfish reverence, homely though it be, of the thousands in my State who to-day occupy farms of broad fertile acres secured to them through the beneficent provisions of the homestead law. They, sir, and the generations that are to come after them, will ever hold in grateful remembrance his manful advocacy of the principles of that law long before its enactment. At a time, sir, when it had few if any friends but himself, and seemingly but little to hope from the future, ANDREW JOHNSON pointed the way, and the republican party, to its honor and its glory be it said, afterward followed therein until this great boon for the homeless and the landless was secured.

Mr. President, I recall to-day a reminiscence of unusual interest to myself, at least. Will you indulge me while I refer to it? On the sixth day of next month fifteen years will have passed since in company with another gentleman, both of us citizens of the then sparsely-settled Territory of Nebraska, I sat in yonder gallery, electrified by the patriotic eloquence of ANDREW JOHNSON. That, as I remember, was my first visit to this Chamber; certainly his great speech for the Union, delivered upon that occasion, was the first to which I ever listened here. On the 5th day of last March I met ANDREW JOHNSON upon this floor, after his long absence from the Senate. We met here then as Senators-elect, and when, together, we swore to uphold the Constitution of our country, my memory went back over the eventful interval of time that had elapsed, and the patriot statesman, who, alone of all his section, had stood bravely up from out the very ranks of secession on yonder side, and, with firm but tearful utterance, proclaimed his unalterable fealty to the Union and the old flag, was again before me. My companion, too, of the gallery was here; I meet him now as my colleague upon this floor; we were here together to represent a

State containing nearly half a million of people, a sovereignty which did not exist when, upon that memorable occasion to which I have adverted, ANDREW JOHNSON denounced secession and disunion with so much power and vehemence; the rebellion had come and gone, bearing its full fruition of direful consequences, as he did then predict; a river of blood had carried between its full banks, upon a resistless tide, the worn and battered hulk of slavery far into the sea of perdition. The Union was restored, re-invigorated by the rich draughts it had drawn fresh from the fountain of liberty, and the great army of American civilization, with "standards full high advanced," was moving forward to new centenary conquests. That, sir, was a moment of intensest interest to my whole nature for the reflections it induced, as this is one of profoundest sorrow for the memories that, crowding mournfully each upon the other, have taken full possession of us all.

Mr. President, I believe, sir, notwithstanding the fact that a painful chapter of history relating to the official acts of ANDREW JOHNSON was made in this very Chamber, that no Senator here present will refuse to-day to join me in the declaration that he was essentially an honest man; ay, sir, a patriot in the fullest sense of the term. It is true, indeed, sir, that he possessed his full share of the weakness by which human nature, wherever found, in its highest as well as its lowest estate, is always beset. And yet, sir, who among *us* will undertake to exalt himself above his fellows in respect of his freedom therefrom? Speaking for myself alone, I do frankly admit that upon sudden impulse, under great excitement, I have spoken words and performed acts which I would gladly expunge from life's record, and thank my God upon bended knees for the opportunity so to do. Who of you, brother Senators, will say less than this for himself? Who of you will undertake to say *more* than this of ANDREW JOHNSON?

To-day, sir, the voice of party is hushed, and the war of factions and policies is forgotten, while, as mourners as of a common brotherhood, we all do pause before the new-made grave of ANDREW JOHNSON to drop the tear of sad remembrance. His ashes now mingle with the soil of the State he loved so well and served so faithfully in the Union he helped to save, but his spirit has gone, with those of Wilson and of Ferry, to unite with those of Lincoln and Seward and the other immortal patriots who went before in that invisible spiritual aggregation whence we are to draw the inspiration which shall quicken here the development and the growth of a higher, a purer civilization, and a stronger, a nobler nationality. God speed the day, sir, when, by the aid of this inspiring influence, the popular sentiment of our country as well as its ethics shall demand of politicians, of statesmen, of parties, and that political power, the press, the exercise of the broadest and the fullest Christian charity in all their intercourse each toward the other.

ADDRESS OF MR BOGY, OF MISSOURI.

Mr. President, having held an important position under Mr. Johnson while he was President of the United States, I was frequently brought in contact with him, and I had for this reason a good opportunity to form an estimate of his abilities and to study the main characteristics of his mind and the great outlines of his general character. A sense of duty, growing out of this official connection, impels me to say a few words on this occasion. I do this with great diffidence, not only because of my inability to do justice to the subject, but also because I follow other Senators who have spoken with much more eloquence than I pretend to possess.

That our late brother was a remarkable man is a fact which is beyond all doubt, and which no one will contest; indeed, his singularly remarkable career is enough to establish this. In my opinion, it is not extravagant to say that this career has no parallel in history in this or any other country, nor in this or any other age of the world. For, although history has preserved and transmitted to us the names of many men born in obscurity and in the humblest station in life who attained the very highest positions in their country, yet in most instances, if not in every one, these men were thrown up as it were by the force of great events with which they were in some way connected, and in most cases these remarkable ascents of men from obscurity to distinction were of military characters. History informs us that several of the emperors of Rome, when it was the mistress of the civilized and barbarian world, were born in slavery. Pizarro, a hog-driver, became the conqueror of Peru, and his name will live in the annals of history forever. And yet it is not difficult to understand the rise of the Roman slave or of the young hog-driver; great events with which they were connected, and which they had the genius to control, made them what they were. But in the case of Mr. JOHNSON his rise from obscurity to distinction through a long gradation of offices and to a seat in this body was the work of his own hands and the legitimate results of his own unaided exertions and great native ability. He was truly the sole architect of his own fortunes. No fortunate or singular circumstances favored his election as alderman of his village nor as mayor, or his election as a member of the Legislature of his State, or to a seat in the House of Representatives of the United States, nor as governor of his State, and finally to a seat in this body as an American Senator. Up to this time it can be truly said that he carved his own fortunes alone and unaided by any adventitious circumstances of any kind. Will, pluck, and ability were the weapons he wielded to accomplish his purposes; and we are informed from his well-known history that he attained the ends which he aimed to accomplish, not by intrigue or cunning, but by a stern and manly course, meeting his opponents and all opposition boldly and defiantly, and so far from attempting to avoid opposition, inviting it Indeed, his combative temper always brought about very great opposition. This he seemed to enjoy. He loved the excitement of a warm political contest, and for it he was most singularly adapted—a ready debater, quick at repartee, a naturally close reasoner, having a profound knowledge of the heart of the people among whom his lot was cast, ready and able to take advantage of any favorable circumstance which presented itself. He went before the people with views and opinions of his own, advocating them boldly and ably, and was always willing and ready to stand or fall with them, and, although a democrat, very seldom, if ever, in line with his party. He was not a demagogue, but he always presented himself as the friend of the people, and particularly of the poor and humble. That in presenting himself on all occasions as the friend of the poor and humble he was honest and sincere, admits of no doubt. His own humble birth and the circumstances surrounding his early years were enough of themselves to impart to his peculiar nature a feeling of sincere love and sympathy for this portion of his fellow-men. He was one of them, and his sympathy for them was natural. And this sympathy he exhibited during his long political life. Yet this by itself would not be sufficient to account for his extraordinary success.

I said at the outset that my official position while he was

President of the United States enabled me to form an estimate of his abilities and of his general character. While his abilities, in my opinion, were not of the very highest order, yet they were very far above the common run of men, and indeed, when his want of early training is considered, they might well be considered as extraordinary. I did not think that his perceptive faculties were very quick, but he possessed great natural power of elaboration, and he worked out his conclusions by serious and laborious thinking. He made the impression on me of a great thinker, and was willing to do a great deal of hard work in this way. When his mind was fully made up he was as firm as a rock, and nothing on earth could shake him. It may be that he indeed carried this too far, and he was in consequence of this considered by some as head-strong and stubborn. His moral courage was great; was, indeed, sublime. I well remember that during the darkest period of his life, when he appeared to be abandoned by all, he never expressed a doubt of his final triumph; and that this was not assumed but was really felt was shown by his deportment and bearing. I have reason to believe that his physical courage was as great as his moral. Hence he was truly and essentially a brave man, willing and ready to risk his life and political fortunes to carry out his object; and in my opinion this had much to do in securing his long life of success.

It is said that he never was at school, not even for a day, and that his wife, who survives him, was his first instructor.

If this be true, his long and successful career must have been a source of great happiness to her, and she must have shared his great and long-continued honors with most singular satisfaction. That his education was under the circumstances imperfect is easily understood; yet he did much to repair this by very general reading. I had occasion to spend many evenings with him, and I then observed that his reading was pretty extensive, although desultory. To say that his memory was good is not enough. At the time I speak of it was truly remarkable, and, as he had served many years in Congress during the days of Calhoun, Clay, Webster, Benton, Grundy, and many others of the distinguished men of that most brilliant period of our history, he could relate many very interesting events connected with them, some of a political nature, some social, and others anecdotical. On such occasions he was extremely genial and amiable, enjoying a hearty laugh as much as any one I ever knew. He possessed good powers of relating past events or anecdotes. I observed one thing, that in speaking of those great men with whom he had become acquainted in this city during his long congressional career, he did so kindly and respectfully, doing full justice to their abilities and to their motives.

Mr. President, it is singular, but it is true, that he filled every office which a man can fill in this country, municipal, State, and Federal, civil and military, judicial, (as mayor,) legislative, and executive, from the lowest to the highest, from alderman of a small village to the governorship of his State, major-general in the Army during the war, and finally Vice-President and President of the United States. The last two offices, however, were not the result, like the others, of his own individual labors. Circumstances growing out of the war had no doubt much to do with his selection as a candidate for the Vice-Presidency, and we all know that a circumstance with which he was in no way connected made him President. But his last election to a seat on this floor as Senator was the work of own hands, brought about by his own indomitable will and pluck, the reward of a long and terrible contest, continuing for some years, unsuccessful for a time, and appearing to all the world besides himself as utterly hopeless; nevertheless, finally he was triumphant. From what I have learned from those who are familiar with this his last contest, he exhibited more openly his true and peculiar nature than at any other period of his life—which was to fight with all his might and all his ability, asking for no quarter and granting none; and although, like bloody Richard, now and then unhorsed, still to fight and never surrender until victory perched on his banner. Under all the circumstances connected with his previous life—particularly while he was the Chief Executive of this country—this last triumph must have given him more sincere and deeply-felt gratification than any other of his life. He is the only one of the number of distinguished men who have held the office of President who afterward became a member of this body. Even in this his fortune appeared to be singular.

I have thus, Mr. President, in a brief and imperfect manner given an outline of the character of this remarkable man. On an occasion like this, and in this body, criticism would be out of place. One of his acts I condemned; but, I repeat, this is neither the occasion nor the place to indulge in criticism. This belongs to history; and his name will be written on its pages and be transmitted to posterity as one of the remarkable characters of our epoch, and as the most perfect type of our republican institutions. His death at this time I consider a public misfortune, as he occupied a position to render great service to his section of our common county.

Distinguished as he was, great as he was, too, his career is ended, and forever; and we again are reminded of the solemn truth that—

The paths of glory lead but to the grave.

### Address of Mr. Jones, of Florida.

Mr. President, when the minister of God on the last day of the previous session of this body invoked the Divine protection over each of its assembled members, I well remember, as I looked over this Chamber, how the thought suggested by the prayer of the holy man came to my mind—shall we all ever meet again on this floor? That mental interrogatory has been answered in the negative, for since our last meeting in this Chamber at the previous session it has pleased Divine Providence to remove from his earthly sphere, from his family, his country, and his usefulness, our distinguished brother-member ANDREW JOHNSON.

It would not be proper for me, Mr. President, an inexperienced member of this body and a comparative stranger to the deceased, to attempt anything like an encomium upon his character and services, or to enlarge upon the just tributes of honor and praise which have been bestowed upon him by those Senators around me who are so well qualified by their talents and their knowledge of his worth and achievements to perform that sad service. Nor is it from a vain desire to have it said that my humble voice has been raised in these most melancholy services to genius and integrity, that I presume to address you now. But, sir, I feel that to be silent on this occasion would be to refuse to the heart the agency of the tongue to relieve it from the emotions of sadness and regret with which the loss of our honored companion has filled me. Not that that loss is to me so personal as to create the pangs of common grief or affliction. There was no tender personal tie between us to be broken. There is nothing in my feelings of regret on this occasion to mark them from those ordinary emotions which the loss of any good man would produce, except, sir, the uncommon fervency and depth which the public character of the misfortune has occasioned. I feel, sir, that, situated as the country is and as this Senate is, the loss of Mr. JOHNSON is great, if not irreparable, and that if he could have lived through the period for which he was elected to this body, the country would have derived great benefit from his services.

In a country like ours, sir, there is no safer or surer way to measure the usefulness or value of a public man than by a consideration of the influence and power which he wields over the minds and hearts of the people Under other systems this influence and power do not produce the same results which they do here. The mysterious councils of despotism seldom consider the temper or the affections of the people; and where the latter take no part in the business of government, except to toil to support its aggressions, there is no field for popular leadership or the operation of that sympathy and influence which we have seen binding the people of this country to their rulers with more than despotic force. It has fallen to the lot, sir, of but few men even in this country to command for any great length of time the pure and unselfish love of the people. Great talents and attainments have always exercised, as they should do, a proper influence over the minds of our citizens, and have ever received the highest favors that the people could bestow. But, sir, in all the tributes and honors bestowed upon the many great intellects of the country, there was very little evidence of affectionate attachment or heartfelt devotion on the part of the people.

But it was not the only merit of Mr. JOHNSON that his mind was distinguished for those qualities which ranked him with men of eminence. Gifted as he was in this respect, he had also that which all men of eminence aim to acquire and but few possess, the power to command and the virtue to merit the love and respect of the people. When we contemplate the career of this wonderful man, commencing at the lowest and rising to the highest stratum of society, by means, and by means only, of his own untiring will and talents, it should afford us great satisfaction and pride to have even this example (if it were all, which it is not) of the good effect of our system of government in opening up to the whole people all the honors and emoluments of the State.

In reviewing the tedious and slow progress of governmental reform, with its relapses and conflicts, sometimes attended with tears and blood and at others breaking down the barriers of time and prejudice with the force of truth and reason, there are no facts which appear more striking in the long march of improvement than the tenacity, the mistrust, and jealousy which were ever exhibited by the enemies of the people in their efforts to withhold from society all interest and influence in its own government.

You cannot but remember the terrible conflict so long maintained at Rome for exclusive privileges by the patricians, and the despair and apprehension with which they ultimately yielded to their fellow-citizens a voice in the management of public affairs. It seems to have been claimed at the very dawn of civilization that the imperfect constitution of man would never be made to harmonize with the principles of regular government, unless the persons who administered it could succeed in deluding the people by a show of authority emanating from some mysterious or divine source. And those grand epochs in the history of human liberty, so often pointed to with pride, only attest the slavery and degradation which surrounded those champions of freedom who looked for the foundation of their rights and privileges in the concessions and charters of kings.

Melancholy and sad as this occasion is, it brings to our minds in the most vivid light the true genius of our own free institutions. The grand figure which surmounts this Capitol may be the work of some man whose conceptions of liberty were inspired by the surroundings of despotism.

Nothing attests the purity and correctness of imagination more than those pictures of art which are drawn with fidelity by one who has never seen the originals. But still they are only pictures. In the life and character and services of him we mourn to-day we have more than a picture. We see reflected before us not the "watery," but the full and living "image" of a free constitution.

It was quite natural for Mr. JOHNSON to feel more than an ordinary attachment for the Union and Constitution of these States. That he did entertain the most sincere devotion for the principles of this Government no one the least disposed to fairness can deny. He felt too strongly the benefits it conferred to be willing to risk its advantages for any other system, and with an honesty and sincerity which commanded even the respect of his foes he clung to it through all its fortunes. If he favored those measures of war which were adopted by the North when war was a real issue, he also favored the cultivation of kindly sentiments toward the South, when it was not popular to sympathize with that war-wasted section. In the unhappy condition of the southern people, this man of bitter prejudices and strong hatred found abundant opportunity to display the bad passions which were said to have possessed him. But, sir, history does not show, Christian charity and meekness the world over do not exhibit, an instance of greater fidelity to principle, a more sublime example of self-abnegation, or a more complete disregard of all selfish interests, than were made manifest in the humane policy of Andrew Johnson toward the South at a time when he had it in his power to oppress her people.

What motives, think you, prompted him to rise, as he did rise, far above the current of sectional hate and prejudice which for years had carried upon their surface the brightest minds and purest hearts in the country? As a Southern man, he was true to the Union; as a lover of the Union, he was true to the Constitution. In maintaining his consistency, he was frequently misrepresented and oftener misunderstood. While supporting the Government, he was accused of having deserted his section; while supporting the Constitution, he was charged with infidelity to the Union and partiality toward the South. He received alternately the praises and condemnation of both sections, and his efforts to serve the country were applauded or denounced as they met the views or crossed the purposes of contending parties. But, regardless of what was thought or said of him, he followed his own stern convictions of duty, and clung to his opinions with more than an Eastern devotion. Among the mountains of Tennessee, imperiled by dangers, he proclaimed his adhesion to the Union. From his high position as President of the United States, he had the courage to speak a kind word for the South and recommend moderation toward her people. If he sought popularity, as it is said he did, he could say with Lord Mansfield that it was not the popularity which is run after, but that which follows in the train of duty fearlessly performed.

For a time he seemed to be lost in the obscurity of popular neglect. The great party which had elevated him to the first position in the Government pursued him with a bitterness and hatred not often exhibited toward political foes.

Who would have supposed that the State whose interests and fortunes he was said to have deserted would again honor him with the highest position in her gift? This was indeed a victory; but it was a victory of fairness and candor over prejudice; of truth over error; of intelligence over ignorance; and of principle over policy. The re-entry of Mr. JOHNSON into this body was a triumph seldom seen in these degenerate days. I speak not now of the *éclat* and popular applause which accompanied it; but I speak of the moral grandeur exhibited in the return to public service of a worthy servant of the people, who, because he would not follow his party when he thought it was in error, was saved by the justice of his former enemies from the condemnation of his friends. A very eminent member of this body, who also, to the great loss of the country, lies cold in death, once said on this floor, while speaking on an occasion like this, that in a celebrated town of Italy there was a fine collection of paintings open to public view. Between two of the most attractive pictures in the room was a large vacant space, evidently intended for some noble work of art, but which was shrouded in deep mourning, which none could penetrate. This veiled mystery attracted more attention than all the paintings in view. So let it be with that part of the history of the illustrious deceased which, for his own and the sake of his country, we could wish should never be written.

Let us hope, sir, that while his example of patience, industry, and success may continue forever to illustrate the greatness of his own virtues and encourage the youth of our country to emulate his fame, his, as it is the first, may remain the last case in our annals in which a President of this great Republic ever appeared as a defendant at your bar.

If any additional sanction were needed to bind us to the strict performance of our high duties here, surely the uncertainty of life and the certainty of death, as shown by the sudden departure of our deceased friend, ought to be sufficient warning to us all to profit well by the hours at our command ere we are overtaken by that night wherein no man can labor.

ADDRESS OF MR. BAYARD, OF DELAWARE.

Mr. President, with the exception of the few weeks of the last special session of the Senate, I had personally no public service in connection with our late associate, ANDREW JOHNSON, of Tennessee; nor had there been at any time intimacy between us, nor had our habits of life been sympathetic. Yet, feeling that his career must be of interest to every American, and his personal qualities and public conduct so full of what was useful to the country and honorable to himself, I have to-day a sad pleasure in bearing testimony above his bier to his worth, and in recalling to his surviving countrymen some of the true lessons of his life, although, perhaps, the full and interesting remarks to which we have listened may make mine superfluous. His career notably illustrated a just and generous feature in our institutions. I mean that very essence of freedom, "*freedom of opportunities*," that "fair field and no favor," upon which every American youth starts in the race of life for success in any profession, for wealth, for fame, for political position and power. In other and less favored lands, of "just and old renown" there is what the poet has well termed the "invidious bar" of humble and obscure birth, which obstructs the timid and inexperienced youth as with unpracticed step he enters upon the rough path of life, and sometimes embarrasses him sadly even to his journey's end. Happily in America this does not exist. Nay, may it not rather be doubted whether the repute of superior fortune and social position is not a weight in the race for popular favor, subjecting their possessor to detraction at the hands of the inconsiderate many?

The man of whom we now speak in his youth was poor, unlettered, and obscure. He had native vigor of mind and body, and the unfettered opportunity afforded by our institutions of government to test freely his capacities in any direction he saw fit. His necessities compelled him to seek employment as a mechanic, and by the labor of his hands he earned his bread; but in all those years of toil he omitted no opportunity or effort to supply the deficiencies in his early education and mental culture. He presented himself as a candidate for public station, and by the suffrages of his fellow-citizens he rose step by step until he became a member of the co-ordinate House of Congress, then of this body, and afterward its presiding officer; then, by an event whose dreadful tragedy shocked the whole country, he became President of the United States.

We live too near the times in which his official action became so important in its influences upon the country to attempt its history. He came to power and place in a stormy period, the excitements of which have not yet entirely subsided, and the serenity and judicial calmness that should mark the page of history will be those of a future generation, whose pulses never thrilled on one side or the other with the passions of the times in which he lived and died.

But part of his life and example may now be properly examined, and examined only to be approved. Friend and foe alike must admit his steady, unshaken love of country; his constant industry; his simple integrity and honesty; his courage of conviction, that never faltered. All these are worthy examples for the emulation of American youth and the youth of all lands. These home-bred virtues induced a life of simplicity and thoughtful economy; kept his hand clean from even a suspicion of improper gain, and in a long public career preserved him from the many temptations that so often warp men of strong passions and vigorous character like his from the path of duty. He possessed and cherished the fine old-fashioned sense of propriety that prevented his acceptance of gifts from any source or of any nature during his tenure of high official power and patronage, even though proffered in the guise of warm personal and patriotic friendship. His performance of public and official duties was marked by industry and constant care.

Qualities and habits such as these surely are entitled to thankful recognition, and being admirable and wholesome, are always examples needed by a people; by none more than those living under a republican form of government; never more than in the times in which we live.

ANDREW JOHNSON's rise and success in life will ever be

an encouragement and incentive to the poor and friendless among his countrymen to cultivate their intellectual faculties; to neglect no opportunity for the best and most important education—*self-education;* to be industrious and frugal, that they may be, and continue to be, honest men; to avoid those extravagant modes of living which create temptations so difficult to resist; to be steadfast in adversity, and ever faithful to the Government which protects them.

Such habits and qualities will almost certainly bring success; but if not success, then something far better and higher than success—self-respect and the respect and esteem of their fellow-men, the consciousness of duty fulfilled to themselves and their country, whose best hopes largely depend upon the formation of such habits and in the exercise of such virtues by its public men.

Address of Mr. Key, of Tennessee.

Mr. President, Andrew Johnson was a very remarkable man. The qualities of his mind and disposition were so unique and peculiar as to lead those acquainted with him to entertain different opinions as to their composition and tendencies.

As is well known, Mr. Johnson's birth was in the midst of poverty and obscurity. His father died when Andrew was but four years old. The son never passed a day in school. At the age of ten years he was apprenticed to a tailor. This species of servitude galled the spirit of the proud boy, and he escaped from it by flight. Unable subsequently to come to terms with his master, he left North Carolina, the State of his nativity, and, crossing its mountains, came to East Tennessee, then a sort of *terra incognita*. In September, 1826, in his eighteenth year, Mr. Johnson arrived at Greeneville, Tenn., accompanied by his mother. An old wooden cart, drawn by a worthless horse, carried all their worldly goods. He could scarcely read, and could not write. Unpromising as the prospect appeared, this youth was destined to address listening Senates, to preside over the destinies of the grandest and greatest republic the world has ever seen, at a most critical period of its history, and to send his name and fame to the farthest limits of civilization.

Born and reared under the most adverse circumstances, it was not possible that the features and general contour of his mind should be shaped in complete harmony or perfect regularity. Something of ruggedness and angularity of mental, moral, and social characteristics must result from such surroundings as encompassed his early life. His poverty and want of education fettered a bold and ambitious spirit, capable of the highest aspirations. The very unequal distribution of advantages doubtless appeared to him in the aspect of a wrong. A restless and longing mind, shackled and imprisoned, is not apt to be always reasonable and just when it discovers, in the pathway through which its aspirations lead, obstacles which seem to be insurmountable, and beholds beyond them those who have been favored by fortune.

Mr. Johnson's associations from his birth to his manhood were with the poor and unlearned. Rising thence by his unaided exertions, he was under no obligation to those who had moved in a sphere superior to his own, and felt none. His sympathies were and they remained with the class of society in which he had been trained. He had not in youth fallen under the refining influences which do so much to soften, enlarge, and diversify man's habitudes and tendencies. His prejudices in favor of the feebler ranks of population became a mental habit before he was able to raise himself into more liberal and enlightened companionship. Of this kinship with the humble he was never ashamed, but it produced in him a distrust of the leaders of society and parties, and led him to the utterance of sentiments on some occasions which were charged to be agrarian in tendency, and caused many to allege that he was a demagogue. Mr. JOHNSON was neither an agrarian nor a demagogue. He never put his trust in princes or courted the favor of party leaders, nor was he loved by them. His whole life was a scene of conflict, and his triumphs were in spite of leaders. His faith was in the people. Them he loved and trusted. He reposed upon their honor, honesty, patriotism, and virtue. His tribunal of last resort was the people, and to them he appealed. When parties and platforms displeased him he turned his back upon them and rallied his countrymen around him. They loved him, and whether he followed party or not they followed him in multitudes.

On the day of his funeral, if one had stood by the grave of our late President, and had seen the procession which came to it with the body of the dead statesman, among the thousands there he would have discovered not many of earth's great ones; not many in office; no display of "pomp and circumstance." A plain hearse carried the remains of the great dead. Two or three carriages held the members of his family. In that vast procession there was no other vehicle. But the people whom Mr. JOHNSON had loved were there. They had gathered from the fields and workshops, from the mountains and the valleys, their faces browned by the sun and their hands hardened by toil. They had all come; the old, those of middle age, the youthful, and the children. There was none of the pageantry and display which usually follow earth's great ones to sepulture, but in their stead were sad faces and tears, such as go only with loved ones to the tomb. In the solemnity of that hour the mountains, which had stood the sentinels of Mr. JOHNSON's home and now look down upon his sepulcher, seemed to join in the general sorrow.

In the beginning of our recent civil struggle Mr. JOHNSON's influence, courage, and activity contributed most powerfully to carry with him a majority of the people of his section of the State in favor of the Federal Union. The authorities of his State, with armies to enforce obedience, were against him, and he had no support at hand but his unarmed and undisciplined multitude; still, unintimidated by threats and unawed by danger, he held aloft the banner of the Union and appealed to the people to uphold it. We know something of the fearful animosities engendered in a community divided in civil war; how the passions are turned loose to deeds of horror at which the blood freezes. Power is used with a remorseless hand, and he who stands in its way is in constant peril.

It was from such a condition of affairs as this, with its hate, revenge, and scenes of blood fresh in his mind, that Mr. JOHNSON entered the presidential chair. I remember well the alarm of the people of the South when the sad news was borne to them of President Lincoln's assassination. Mr. JOHNSON's denunciations of those who had opposed the Federal Government, and the punishment and penalties he had invoked and threatened, justified the gravest apprehensions. But when he came to be President; when his enemies had laid down their arms and furled their flag, and after the power to pardon as well as to punish had passed into his hands, satisfied, as he must have been, that the great mass of the Southern people had been honest, though mistaken, as he believed, in the motives which had impelled their action, all his bitterness and acrimony toward them were dissipated. The man sank himself out of sight, and the President of a powerful nation shielded his late foes by his clemency, though the liberal policy he exercised toward them contributed powerfully to lose him the support of the party which had placed him in office. He who could exercise such magnanimity under such circumstances had a great heart and unflinching fortitude. Those who think Mr. JOHNSON was cold and very selfish never understood his inner nature.

In many respects he was strange and peculiar, so that it is no matter of surprise that many who did not fully comprehend him had an unfavorable estimate of some of the qualities of his mind and heart. He was combative, and always armed and equipped for the fray. He did not wait to be assailed, but was usually the first to enter the lists, and no matter how great the odds against him, or how formidable the antagonist, he was eager for the contest. He was also aggressive. He chose to carry the war into the enemy's territory, and it was hard to drive him to a defensive attitude; nor would he leave the field until he had won a complete victory or had suffered a decisive defeat. His life was a contest, and his love of fight sometimes precipitated him into controversies which had been better avoided. He was fearless, self-reliant, and bold, and never bent "the pregnant hinges of the knee where thrift may follow fawning."

Mr. JOHNSON was an honest man. He was never accused of duplicity or unfair dealing. His errors resulted from his convictions of right. Though for forty years he was in the public service, and often in situations in which gratuities and bribes might have been accepted or public funds appropriated with little fear of detection, yet no stain of official corruption had soiled his hands or life. Frugality was a habit with him, and yet out of his salaries in public life he saved only a fair competence.

There were two central ideas around which all his political views revolved, and to which his actions were subordinated. He regarded the Constitution, State and Federal, with a veneration and devotion of kin to fanaticism. He appealed to the Constitution on all occasions and under all circumstances, was constantly in apprehension of its violation, and everywhere held it up before the assemblies and tribunals of the nation, and demanded that every jot and tittle of it be observed. With him it was the ark of our safety, as sacred and privileged as was that ark of Israel which could not be touched by profane hands. No measure, howsoever great in its expediency or utility, could receive his support or sanction unless it had certain warrant in the Constitution. His other grand idea was confidence in the people and a strict regard for the protection and security of their interests and the preservation of their liberties. Amplify his theory as he might, these ideas composed its substance. He feared the encroachments of the Government upon the rights of the people. The times of the Cæsars, when the republic of Rome was transformed into an empire, and of the Charleses of England, when the prerogatives of the crown were extended and enlarged at the expense of the liberties of the people, were with him favorite fields of history, which he carefully explored and often referred to as exhibiting the dangers which threaten a civilized free government.

Mr. JOHNSON's skill was not so much in construction as in resistance to the schemes and measures of others. His great desire and aim were to maintain and preserve what our fathers had handed down to us. He was afraid that change might mar their work.

Mr. JOHNSON will be a marvel in history. His ascent from the lowest station in society, without adventitious aids or fortunate accidents, and with surroundings the most unpromising, to the grand elevation he attained, cannot be understood and appreciated in any land but ours, and it is an astonishing consummation in it, furnishing splendid evidence of the value, power, and glory of our institutions. He will be held up to the ages to come as an illustrious example of what the poorest and obscurest boy may accomplish if he but have perseverance, pluck, and capacity.

Another shining example of this class is found in him who so lately, Mr. President, filled with so much distinction the chair in which you sit to-day.

Mr. JOHNSON has gone from this presence and this Chamber, and will return no more. The "insatiate archer" has no respect for persons, station, or rank. The king and the peasant, the president and the beggar alike become his victims; but, among all the country's dead, this Government has never lost, and never will lose, a more loyal and fearless defender or its people a more devoted friend than ANDREW JOHNSON.

The resolutions were adopted unanimously, and the Senate (at 2 o'clock and 38 minutes p. m.) adjourned.

PROCEEDINGS

IN THE

HOUSE OF REPRESENTATIVES.

# ANNOUNCEMENT.

A message was received from the Senate, by Mr. McDonald, its Chief Clerk, which informed the House of the proceedings in that body upon the announcement of the death of Hon. ANDREW JOHNSON, late a Senator from the State of Tennessee.

The SPEAKER. The Clerk will read the resolutions just received from the Senate.

The Clerk read as follows:

*Resolved, unanimously,* That the Senate has received with profound sorrow the announcement of the death of Hon. ANDREW JOHNSON, late a Senator of the United States from the State of Tennessee.

*Resolved, unanimously,* That as a mark of respect for the memory of Mr. JOHNSON, the members of the Senate will go into mourning by wearing crape upon the left arm for thirty days.

*Resolved, unanimously,* That as an additional mark of respect for the memory of Mr. JOHNSON, the Senate do now adjourn.

*Resolved,* That the Secretary communicate these resolutions to the House of Representatives.

# ADDRESSES.

### Address of Mr. McFarland, of Tennessee.

Mr. Speaker, the duty devolves on me, as the Representative of the first congressional district of Tennessee, to announce to the House the death of a distinguished citizen of Tennessee, whose home, from his first appearance in that State in 1826 to the day of his death, was in the congressional district I have the honor to represent in this House. I allude to the death of Hon. Andrew Johnson, late a Senator from Tennessee, Ex-President of the United States, and for ten years a member of this House, which occurred at the residence of his daughter, Mrs. Brown, in Carter County, Tennessee, on the morning of the 31st of July last.

Mr. Johnson was called to his final account and closed his connection with time and earthly things without that protracted sickness and suffering which gives premonition of approaching dissolution. He was stricken with paralysis a day or two previous to his death, and almost as soon as his sickness was known the melancholy tidings were flashed to the most distant parts of our country that Andrew Johnson was dead. Not to our country only, but to the whole civilized world abroad, was the sad intelligence carried with lightning speed that the "Great Commoner" was no more.

His remains were interred on a lofty eminence west of the town of Greeneville, a spot selected by himself, commanding an extended view of the surrounding country, and there, amid those mountain heights, all that is mortal of ANDREW JOHNSON is crumbling into dust. The voice that has been so often heard in this Chamber is silenced forever. The form that was so familiar in these halls has disappeared, and will be seen no more. Shrouded in the flag of his country, beneath the shadow of which he fought the great political battles of his life, and whose triumphant folds were ever to him an object of adoration which he worshiped with an unswerving devotion, far from the din and strife and turmoil of the outer world, he quietly sleeps that last, long, peaceful sleep which knows no waking.

ANDREW JOHNSON's career as a public man is the most remarkable and wonderful in all our history, and is perhaps unprecedented in modern times. It cannot be expected in the few brief remarks we are to submit to the House now that justice can be done to Mr. JOHNSON's public life, or that we can take more than a glance at a few of the prominent facts in his history.

Mr. JOHNSON was born in Raleigh, N. C., on the 29th day of December, 1808. His father died when he was a child, leaving the future statesman to the care of a widowed mother in poverty and obscurity. At ten years of age he was apprenticed to a tailor in his native town. He was then unable to read, and his first efforts to learn were made during this apprenticeship. A gentleman read to him some sketches from an old book known as "The American Speaker." These extracts aroused the attention of the poor apprentice and first fired his ambition. He determined and did learn to read them for himself. That book was presented to him, and is still preserved in the library of Mr. JOHNSON.

In the fall of the year 1826, on the evening of a dark, gloomy day, a two-wheeled cart, drawn by a blind pony, was driven into the village of Greeneville, East Tennessee, from the direction of the mountains of North Carolina. With it were two men and a woman. The younger of the two, who drove the pony, stopped at the house of a citizen whose sons are now living in that town, and asked for forage to feed his horse, which he procured, and then inquired for suitable camping-ground for the night, to which he drove and encamped, near where now stands the mansion of the Johnson family. In a little less than forty years from that night that homeless wanderer, then about eighteen years of age, shrouded in obscurity and poverty, a stranger in a strange land, without the rudiments of a common education, camping out under the broad canopy of the heavens in the village of Greeneville, became the occupant of the building at the far end of this avenue, and the chief executive officer of a great confederacy of States numbering forty million people! That youth was ANDREW JOHNSON. Such was his first appearance in Tennessee, and thus the first night ANDREW JOHNSON passed in Greeneville, which became his future home.

Mr. JOHNSON established himself in business as a tailor. By his industry, energy, unswerving integrity, and promptness he was successful. As a mechanic, that fidelity to duty and unquestioned honesty which characterized him in every period of his history won for him the confidence and respect of the people, and made him, even then, a power in the community. He was married shortly after he settled in Greeneville, where his widow survives him. She taught him to write; she aided him by her intelligence and instruction in his efforts to acquire the rudiments of an education, and thus laid the foundation of his future greatness. Conscious of his powers and with unfaltering confidence in himself, identified in interest and sympathy with the laboring masses, he applied himself with untiring industry, under disadvantages of a most extraordinary character, to the acquisition of an education and to preparation for his future wonderful career.

In 1828 he was elected an alderman of the village; was re-elected in 1829 and 1830; and was elected to the office of mayor in 1830. He was appointed a trustee of Rhea Academy about 1831; was a member of the lower house of the Tennessee Legislature in 1835. Being defeated in 1837, he was re-elected in 1839. He was elected State senator in 1841, and a member of this House in 1843, to which position he was re-elected for the four succeeding terms. He was elected governor of Tennessee in 1853, re-elected in 1855, and in 1857 was chosen as a Senator in Congress from the State of Tennessee for the term ending March 3, 1863; was appointed military governor of Tennessee during the late civil war in 1862; was a candidate for Vice-President on the ticket with Mr. Lincoln in 1864, to which office he was elected, and by an event never to be forgotten in the history of the country, Mr. JOHNSON, on the 15th of April, 1865, became President of the United States.

Of the events of Mr. JOHNSON's administration I shall not speak. The history of his administration is now part of the history of the country. Posterity will do him justice. The great statesmen of the past have been called to the administration of public affairs in times of peace, when the ship of state was sailing over a calm, unruffled sea. Mr. JOHNSON took the helm in the midst of a storm lashed into fury unprecedented in the history of our country by the angry passions, the bitterness, and strife of a long and bloody civil conflict. To say that he committed no errors would be to say that he was more than human. Now that he has passed away none can gainsay the honesty and integrity of ANDREW JOHNSON, or doubt his unfaltering fidelity to the great principle of constitutional liberty.

After the close of his term as President, in 1869, Mr. JOHNSON returned to his home in Tennessee. He became a candidate for Senator, but was defeated. In 1872, at the demand of a large number of his people, he became a candidate for Congress from the State at large, but was for the third time in the whole course of his public life again defeated. In January, 1875, at the demand of the people, he was elected by the Legislature of Tennessee a Senator in Congress for six years. His last and only appearance in that body after his election was at the extra session in March, 1875, and with the close of that session terminated ANDREW JOHNSON's public services.

Such is a brief statement of the public positions held by Mr. JOHNSON. He was continuously in the public service for almost forty years.

It may be well said that his career was the most wonful in our history. Who, indeed, was ever like him? Who ever, as he did, proved his honesty, his aims, and his ambitions by conquering for them their indisputable vindication? Taking the history of the three-score and seven years of ANDREW JOHNSON, the poverty of his childhood, the neglect of his youth, his humble origin, his growth to manhood without even the rudiments of education, his humble mechanical pursuit, and then looking to his subsequent remarkable career, and we have the outlines of a great man struggling against misfortune, battling against fate, with bitter opposition at every step of his progress, finally conquering every adverse element, and at last elevating himself to the highest position in the Republic.

The poor, uneducated youth became a Senator in Congress, the governor of a great State, and the chief executive of a proud nation; and, dying, has embalmed his memory in the grateful hearts of millions of his countrymen; and, though his form has disappeared, ANDREW JOHNSON lives and will ever live in the affections of the people while the principles of constitutional liberty are cherished, and honesty, integrity, and patriotism, and abilities of the highest order, are venerated by men. Of him it may be said—

> *These* shall resist the empire of decay
> When time is o'er and worlds have passed away:
> Cold in the dust the perished heart may lie,
> But that which warmed it once can never die.

ANDREW JOHNSON was but a man; he had his faults; he committed errors; but, looking to the unfavorable circumstances by which his youth was surrounded, the bitter and continuous political battles in which he was engaged from early life down to his death, the wonder is that he committed so few.

He had his enemies, and his life and history furnish most striking evidence of the truth of the poet's sentiment:

> He who ascends to mountain-tops shall find
>     The loftiest peaks most wrapt in clouds and snow:
> He who surpasses or subdues mankind
>     Must look down on the hate of those below.
> Though high above the sun of glory glow,
>     And far beneath the earth and ocean spread,
> Round him are icy rocks, and loudly blow
>     Contending tempests on his naked head,
> And thus reward the toils which to those summits led.

But Mr. JOHNSON had his friends and admirers, who adhered to him through every vicissitude of his political fortunes, and with the laboring masses of the people of the country perhaps no public man of his day had more influence and power than did he. He was one of them; knew their wants, and sympathized with their struggles.

The life of Andrew Johnson is an example of the lasting fame that surely awaits the honest statesman. His unswerving integrity; his bold, independent, and candid declaration of his opinion on public questions; his confidence in the people, and the absence of disguise in all his acts, were his master-key to the popular heart. The country was never in doubt as to his opinions and purposes, and victorious or defeated, he remained firm in his belief. In all the contests of his time his position on great public questions was as clear as the sun in a cloudless sky.

Sirs, standing by the grave of Andrew Johnson, and looking back over the history of his life and considering these things, how insignificant and contemptible appear the labor and ambition of the mere politician! What a reproach is his life on that false policy which would trifle with a great people! If I were to write the epitaph of Andrew Johnson I would inscribe on the stone which shall mark his resting-place, as the highest eulogy, "Here lies the man who was in the public service for forty years, who never tried to deceive his countrymen, and died, as he lived, 'an honest man, the noblest work of God.'" While the youth of America should imitate his noble qualities, they may take courage from his example, and note the high proof it affords that under our equal institutions the avenues to the highest position are open alike to all.

Mr. JOHNSON rose by the force of his own genius, indomitable will, and untiring energy, unaided by power, prestige, or wealth. At an age when our young men are usually in pursuit of education at institutions of learning, he, in ignorance and poverty, made his way from the "Old North State" toward the West, and, amid the rude collisions incident to East Tennessee at that day, commenced his early struggle, and in less than fifty years matured a character the highest exhibitions of which were destined to mark eras in his country's history. Beginning in the mountains of East Tennessee in 1826, brought into antagonism with the power, influence, and wealth of old citizens of the country, supported by the consciousness of his own powers and by the confidence of the people, he surmounted all the barriers of adverse fortune and won a glorious name in the annals of his country.

Let the generous youth fired with an honorable ambition remember that our American system of government offers on every hand and opens wide the doors to the most exalted position and the grandest reward to merit. If, like ANDREW JOHNSON, orphanage, obscurity, and poverty shall oppress him; yet, if, like him, he feels the Promethean spark within, let him remember that his country, like a generous mother, opens wide her arms to welcome every one of her children whose genius may promote her prosperity or add to her renown. Mr. Speaker, I offer the following resolutions:

The Clerk read as follows:

*Resolved*, That the House of Representatives of the United States has received with the deepest sensibility and profound sorrow the intelligence of the death of Hon. ANDREW JOHNSON, late a Senator from the State of Tennessee, Ex-President of the United States and long a member of this House.

*Resolved*, That the proceedings of this House in relation to the death of Hon. ANDREW JOHNSON be communicated to the widow and family of the deceased by the Clerk of this House.

*Resolved*, That as a further mark of respect for the memory of the deceased this House do now adjourn.

ADDRESS OF MR. WADDELL, OF NORTH CAROLINA.

Mr. SPEAKER: I have been struck since these proceedings commenced with the peculiar circumstances of this occasion. There is to a man who believes in special providences food for reflection in the fact that just as we have reached the climacteric of a debate upon the question whether the American people shall live together as brothers, whether there shall be a government of love or hate, we are suddenly arrested by the remembrance that there is a time appointed for all men once to die. Mr. Speaker, when that supreme hour comes for you and me and for each of us, I know nothing will give us more consolation than the memory of deeds of charity and good-will.

The very remarkable man whose death has just been formally announced to this House was, like many other men who obtained eminence in other States, a native and, until his early manhood, a resident of North Carolina. It is therefore meet, sir, that in this hour dedicated to his memory the voice of that State should be heard, and the duty of uttering it has been assigned to me.

My personal acquaintance with Mr. JOHNSON was very limited and merely formal. I will not therefore undertake to portray his character as a private citizen, nor shall I attempt any sketch of his public life and his varied and distinguished public services, because that has been already done by my friend who has just taken his seat, and is familiar to all more or less.

But he exhibited throughout his public career some qualities upon which brief comment may justly be made, and perhaps not unprofitably at this time. His education, socially and politically, differed in almost every respect from my own. Indeed I might say they were almost antipodal, and never until his memorable struggle, when President, for the preservation of constitutional liberty, as I believe, had any portion of his career attracted my sympathy. But aside from the characteristics which he developed in that struggle he exhibited certain virtues as a public man which must always command respect and admiration—virtues which, if they are not rare nowadays, are certainly not the commonest attributes of those who occupy distinguished station.

Mr. JOHNSON was an honest man, a truthful man, and incorruptible. He obstinately adhered to the opinion which ought to be, but is not, universally accepted and acted upon, that personal integrity and political dishonesty are absolutely irreconcilable in the same person. In all the bitter contests through which he passed, (and his career in this respect is almost without a parallel,) his worst enemy, so far as I know, never attempted to prove, if he ever charged, that ANDREW JOHNSON was a corrupt man.

Whatever his faults, or vices if you please—and, I presume, like all other men, he had his full share of them—he unquestionably had intense convictions, to which he clung with fearless devotion and for which he battled with manly courage. Among these, sir, none were more conspicuous than his faith in the doctrines of the fathers touching the limitations of the Constitution and his firm belief in the maxim that purity of administration is essential to the life of free government.

If his almost fanatical love of the Union caused him at times to assent to the use of arbitrary power, he still always proclaimed the supremacy of the Constitution. If corruption in administration occurred during his Presidency, no one ever accused him of being even remotely connected with it. He at least understood the principles and sympathized with the spirit of republican institutions. He did not think that personal comfort and pecuniary benefit were the chief ends to be aimed at in seeking public offices. He did not accept them at the hands of his countrymen as a debt due to him, and did not administer them, as small men always do, in accordance with his personal feelings and interests. He considered himself the servant of the people, bound by his oath to be careful and diligent in looking out, not for his own, but for their interests. He never was one of those who were called, and aptly called in the civil-service-commission report, "the banditti of politics and the pawnbrokers of patronage."

He may not have been a broad-minded statesman, in

the ordinary acceptation of that term, but it is to be remembered that in his youth there was no opportunity afforded him for broad culture, and that he did not even have a patron to secure for him education at the public expense. He certainly was not a classical scholar. It would seem that he did not even know what *nepos* meant, and was utterly insensible to the charm that lies hidden behind the words *dona ferentes*. But in practical ability, in power as a debater, whether before popular assemblies or legislative assemblies, and in extensive information in the domain of politics, he was by no means deficient. His long and active public service in association with some of the wisest and ablest statesmen of this land, improved, enlarged, and liberalized his naturally powerful intellect to a degree which may perhaps justify his assignment to a place among the ablest of our Chief Magistrates, and certainly to one very far above some of them.

After his death some pious investigator, I believe, claimed to have discovered that he was an infidel. I have very good evidence to disprove that; but while personally I know not how that may have been, I do know that while he was alive and in office he was too good a patriot to seek to excite a religious persecution against any portion of his fellow-citizens. If he had religious views of any kind, it is safe to say that they were his own, and were arrived at after mature deliberation and reflection; but whatever they were, sir, he never sought to make political capital out of them.

Mr. Speaker, ANDREW JOHNSON has gone to his long rest, as sooner or later each and all of us must go. After a long and laborious career, begun in poverty, ignorance, and friendlessness, but crowned throughout its course with earthly honors, he now confronts the mysteries of eternity. It may possibly be some consolation to his friends to believe that if for his deeds done in the body he be impeached in his new state of existence, he will at least have angels for his prosecutors and the Merciful One for his judge. That is the only consolation that is left to any of us in contemplating the events of a future life.

I do not hold up Mr. JOHNSON as an exemplar either in morals or in politics. Very few are the men to whom I could pay that tribute. But, sir, the qualities which I have ascribed to him, and which he possessed, may well be emulated by some of his contemporaries upon whom fortune or an inscrutable Providence has devolved the duties and responsibilities of public office. Upon many of them have more brilliant gifts been bestowed. They have been more learned, more eloquent, more popular than he. But not of every one of them can it be said, as of him, he was honest, he was truthful, he was incorruptible. These are traits, sir, which his native State of North Carolina will never cease to honor in any American statesman, whether born within her borders or not. And therefore, as a tribute to them, as developed in ANDREW JOHNSON, she now lays her wreath upon his tomb.

ADDRESS OF MR. THORNBURGH, OF TENNESSEE.

Mr. Speaker, representing in part that section of the State of Tennessee which was the home of ANDREW JOHNSON, I desire to express my respect for his character and veneration for his memory. My colleague has mentioned the incidents of the early life and the long public career of ANDREW JOHNSON with an interesting completeness that renders unnecessary further recital. Yet an expression of sorrow for his loss, and appreciation for the great virtues he, as a man and a statesman, possessed, cannot be inappropriate, coming from one who, though differing upon political questions, enjoyed his friendship from childhood.

My earliest recollections of political contests and public discussions is connected with the conflicts and triumphs which so characterized his history. There was a period of his life when I had almost daily opportunities to study his character and observe the manner in which he performed important and arduous duties that devolved upon him. This was when Mr. JOHNSON was military governor of Tennessee. It was the stormiest day of our national history. The country was in the midst of civil war, and there are few of us here who have forgotten what civil war means. In this important and responsible position he exhibited many of those great qualities which made him a fit ruler in times of disorder and turbulence. He was fertile in resources, zealous, earnest, and faithful. There were no precedents to guide him in the arduous duties of his office. His vigorous mind, resolute purpose, strong will, were necessary in the work required, while that work itself illustrated his love of justice, his courage, energy, and patriotism. War had almost obliterated all traces of government in Tennessee. The State was a chaos, out of which he was to bring order. The desolation of contending armies made it necessary for him to create supplies, house the homeless, clothe the naked, feed the poor. The courts were closed to the redress of grievances, and justice was to be administered by him. Thousands of Union people flocked to him, begging for supplies and arms. And yet he proved equal to the task before him. He was civil chief magistrate, a general, judge, and quartermaster, and a benefactor of the poor. He worked with constant, tireless energy, bringing order out of confusion, re-instating the courts of justice, redressed grievances, and fed, sheltered, and clothed the homeless poor, without regard to the Army in which their natural protectors might be found. From the Union men around him he raised an army and sent them to the field, where they did gallant service for the Government; and when the capture of his capital was threatened, he refused to abandon it with our retreating Army, but, stern and unfaltering, stood a bulwark for its defense.

But all this has become a part of the history of the country. ANDREW JOHNSON never faltered in his devotion to the Union. With unsurpassed earnestness he devoted every faculty of body and mind to a successful re-establishment of a united republic, looking forward anxiously to the hour when he could bring his State back into the Union and could see her star once more emblazoned on his country's banner. The most notable features in ANDREW JOHNSON's life and character were his humble origin, his utter want of early education, his faithful devotion to the principles he espoused, his great courage and indomitable will. To these circumstances in his history and these traits in his character can be traced, in my opinion, the two most important events in his life. Without these characteristics he might not have stood on the floor of the Senate the solitary representative from the seceding States, and have made that memorable speech on the 27th of July, 1861, which was so full of the deepest political reseach and the most thorough and unselfish patriotism. Starting with the maxim that "*Salus respublicæ suprema lex*," he said:

> The time has come when the Government should put forth its entire power and sustain the supremacy of the Constitution and laws made in pursuance thereof. If we have no government, let the delusion be dispelled, let the dream pass away, and let the people of the United States and the nations of the earth know at once we have no government. If we have a government based on the intelligence and virtue of the American people, let that great fact be now established; and when once established, this Government will be on a more enduring and permanent basis than it ever was before. I still have confidence in the integrity, the virtue, the intelligence, and the patriotism of the great mass of the people; and so believing, I intend to stand by the Government of my fathers to the last extremity.

Sentiments like these, coming at that peculiar crisis in the country's history from a Southern Senator, re-echoed through the land, and gave rebuke to those who could find no power in the Constitution for national self-preservation, and infused new confidence and courage to those preparing for the great conflict that was so soon to follow.

But while ANDREW JOHNSON was resolute in war, no sooner had the echoes of the last battle died away than he became an earnest advocate of a reunited people. He sought to bury all past animosities, and to cultivate the nobler feelings of kindness, forgiveness, and fraternal love. Few men in history could have held the reins of government as its chief executive at that time, when human passions had become inflamed by the memories of this recent terrible war, and have determined the novel and anomalous questions presented without encountering the antagonism of some leading statesmen, and inviting that bitter denunciation of calumny and vilification which now seems to be visited upon all who have attained to exalted position, and who have rendered great services to their country and to mankind. His marked individuality, great tenacity of purpose, and iron will, brought him his full measure of honest opposition and malignant aspersion. But even the genius of slander itself had not the audacity to charge ANDREW JOHNSON with dishonesty in any act of his long and eventful public life.

I shall leave it for others, his contemporaries and associates, to speak more in detail of his career while in the two Houses of Congress and while President of the nation.

A great leader of the people, an orator possessing peculiar power to inspire, persuade, convince, and control the honest masses of the country, has passed the opening portals of the grave, and none feel his loss more keenly or lament his death more sincerely than the humbler classes, from whose ranks he sprang and whose peculiar champion he never ceased to be. His dust now mingles with that of Jackson and Polk in the bosom of Tennessee. Peace to his ashes, honor to his memory.

>Let him rest; it is not often
>  That his soul hath known repose.
>Let him rest; they rest but seldom
>  Whose successes challenge foes.
>He was weary, worn with watching;
>  His life-crown of power hath pressed
>Oft on temples sadly aching;
>  He was weary, let him rest.

ADDRESS OF MR. CONGER, OF MICHIGAN.

Mr. Speaker, in this age of the world the development and character of the individual man is the result of generations of human growth. The victories of the warrior, the achievements of the statesman, and the fanciful creations of the poet are made possible by the existing conditions of society, and are so evoked from and commingled with the innumerable circumstances of human progress as to render it uncertain to what extent they originate in the individual intellect and will, and how far they are the result of myriad unseen agencies.

In the dawn of human existence man, himself a new-wrought miracle, without revelation or tradition, wandered amid the marvels of a new creation to wonder, admire, and adore. We can scarcely realize through what centuries he must have passed from that primitive period of child-like simplicity and instinctive adoration, through the slow development of the idea of the heroic, the beautiful, the religious, and the practical, until he could comprehend the laws of the physical and intellectual world, and tower among millions of the human race the type and representative of the marvelous civilization of the nineteenth century! Every age has marked man's progress, and every great advance in mental and moral culture has had some typical representative of the aggregate development of his social and moral attributes.

On this occasion we pause for a moment in the busy avocations of life to pay the tribute of our respect to the memory of one of our distinguished compeers, who, having exemplified almost every vicissitude of earthly fortune, having attained the highest place of power, and having afterward entered upon a pathway untrodden by any predecessor, has obeyed the inexorable mandate—to rest from his labors on earth.

I have thought, sir, while other gentlemen portrayed his life and character more accurately and eloquently than I have the ability to do, it might not be inappropriate for me to refer to some peculiarities in the life and character of this distinguished citizen which illustrate conditions of fortune that could only exist in American civilization and under American institutions.

Sir, I have believed from early youth, with emotions of pride and gratitude which I have no language to express, that we live in an age and are citizens of a country whose laws, policy, and free institutions, in their true intention and result, opened to every child of the Republic alike the royal road to education, culture, distinction, and honor—the royal highway that leads to everything and all things that are garnered in our grand inheritance of freedom to which the immortal soul might honorably aspire, across which arrogance should build no barricade and ignorance no trench; where wealth should never jostle the poor nor pride override the humble; where virtue might pass with fearless step and devotion might worship at every wayside shrine!

With such reflections, Mr. Speaker, I commend to my countrymen the study of the life and character of ANDREW JOHNSON as illustrating more distinctly than any other example which now occurs to my memory the spirit, the tendencies, and the possibilities of American institutions.

Neither the occasion nor my own inclination will permit more than a brief reference; but the American citizen may inquire with pride, Where else could the child of poverty and ignorance, under like circumstances, have risen to the highest honors of the State? In what other land and under what other civilization could woman have become at once the wife and the teacher of the wandering mechanic, and, accompanying and encouraging his upward progress to honor and power, could have imparted to her daughters such delicate culture and gentle training that, even amid the splendors of the Capital and the throngs of beauty, they could disarm envy by their virtues and excite admiration by their simplicity?

Under what other division of power between the General Government, the States, and the people, could the subject of an impeachment and prosecution the most remarkable and determined ever witnessed in our land have undergone so fiery an ordeal, and afterward so far commanded the respect of political friends and foes that his return to the Senate should meet with general approval?

That he was gifted with remarkable powers none will deny. With a strong intellect, untiring industry, an indomitable will, and an ambition that gathered intensity alike from defeat and success; with little of that personal sympathy which could control the multitude by its electric influence, and with a directness and obstinacy arising in part from physical organization, but more from the mental habitudes peculiar to the varied circumstances of his condition, his life exhibits a greater variety of the phases of character that spread all the way from unworthy littleness to moral grandeur than that of any other statesman whose name illustrates American history.

He was considerate in his friendships, vindictive in his enmities, unforgiving of injury, but moderate in victory. With a blunt honesty of purpose and acknowledged integrity of character, he marshaled his forces, and controlled the situation more through an involuntary respect and an undefined fear than from personal favor and affection.

Remembering his early life, he was ever the friend of the poor, from whose ranks he had risen, yet lacked the loftiness of soul which would have prevented his taking an unworthy pride in humbling the pretensions of wealth and the ostentation of birth.

His zeal for the homeless and landless poor never flagged, and his indomitable love of the Union and struggles for the perpetuity of free institutions challenge the admiration of the world; and even his ceaseless reiterations of his love of the Constitution, although exciting the ridicule of political opponents, were in harmony with his life-long actions and professions.

Sir, there were occasions in his life, rendered sublime by his heroic courage and indomitable zeal for the honor, the Union, and the Constitution of his country, which history will emblazon upon its pages; and when the prejudices and passions of the hour shall have passed away, posterity will inscribe them upon his monument.

Even-handed justice will attribute his foibles and faults to his early struggles with poverty and toil, the imperfection of early culture and education, and to the anomalous condition of the social organization in the midst of which he lived; while the memory of his countrymen will linger around those nobler manifestations of his courage and patriotism in preserving those glorious institutions that invited him from the depths of ignorance and want to the high places of usefulness and honor.

His illustrious example will quicken the genius and stimulate the energy of ten thousand children of poverty and toil to strive for higher culture and search for nobler fields of usefulness and honor, and it may admonish the patriot and statesman with renewed emphasis, that in the more perfect education and virtue of all the people lies the only safe reliance for the perpetuity of our free institutions and the future glory of our country.

Sir, there are nobler things in life than wealth and power; there are far richer treasures for the citizens than lie hidden in the mine, for neither the vast outlines of our domain nor the illimitable wealth within its borders, neither the grandeur of our encircling mountains nor the beauty of our silver streams, neither rapidly-multiplying States, populous cities, nor the unrivaled expanse of rural cultivation can awaken in the breast such emotions of pride and patriotism as the unfaltering belief that through all and over all this glorious land are established such laws and such institutions as will preserve forever, as the irreversible inheritance of the American people, "the absolute equality of manhood and the universal enjoyment of equal rights."

ADDRESS OF MR. YOUNG, OF TENNESSEE.

Mr. Speaker, in the hour of grief, in the ministrations of affliction, when the sable drapery of mourning is drawn in heavy folds around us, and the mind is overshadowed with gloom, silence is sometimes more eloquent and impressive than the chaste rhetoric of the scholar or the flowing declamation of the orator.

In the ceremonies of sorrow, in the expressions of regret and honor to the dead, the downcast face and drooping eye sometimes speak the emotions of the heart in language more touching and truthful than the studied and polished utterances of the eulogist or the glowing phrases clothed in the beautiful imagery of the poet.

After what has been so fittingly and eloquently said by my colleagues who have just spoken, I might with propriety keep my place among the silent spectators of these solemn and impressive ceremonies without by speaking incurring the risk of detracting aught from the beauty of the tributes which they have offered to the memory and public services of the distinguished citizen of our State whose death has just been formally announced to this body; and, indeed, I should have stood reverently, sadly, but in silence before the altar of the people's sorrow, this day unveiled in the council-chamber of the nation, but for the reason that had I done so I should not have reflected the wishes nor met the expectations of a large number of those who clothed me with the honors of an American legislator and sent me here to speak in their name.

But in the little which I shall say expressive of their and my own estimate of the character of the distinguished man whose fortunes they followed with equal courage in the gloom of defeat and the brightness of success, I shall not exaggerate his virtues by the extravagant laudations of the friendly eulogist, nor unveil his faults with the hostile hand of the carping critic. The one is the task of the orator upon the rostrum, the poet in song, and the enthusiast in history, while the other is the congenial work of those who forget the good and remember only the evil that men do, and never learn to cast the mantle of charity even over the graves of those with whom they have struggled in life.

Of great men, whether living or dead, the truth may be fitly spoken. The scales in which their character is weighed may be held with an impartial hand, no matter whether good or evil disturb the equal poise.

ANDREW JOHNSON, when living, was not wont to shrink from any combat nor quail before any foe; and now that he is dead, and the story of his checkered life is passing into history, there is perhaps but little cause to invoke the eulogy of his friends or to supplicate the forbearance of his enemies. To say that he was a perfect man, that no fault marred the symmetry of his character, that no error of action, no weakness or vice of nature dimmed the luster of his fame, would be to raise him above the level of humanity and clothe him with attributes not found in the history of mankind. But as the purest gold is alloyed with baser metal, as some ingrain flaw dims the sparkling light of the rarest jewel, so the fame of the most exalted human character is shadow by some human frailty.

The page upon which the future historian shall record the career and achievements of ANDREW JOHNSON will be fraught with deeper interest to the thoughtful mind than almost any other in the great volume of American history. The story of his life, from the time he laid aside the implements of the humble artisan, through all the gradations of political preferment until the day, only a little while ago, when he was laid in the grave, is a record of bold conception, high aims, grand struggles, and marvelous triumphs.

To relate his struggles and his successes, his combats and his victories, would fill the pages of many volumes; to even group together without comment the grander and more dramatic events of his wonderful career, from the humble workshop of the country village to the stately mansion of the nation's rulers, would extend my remarks beyond the limits fixed by the proprieties of this occasion.

Reaching the period of manhood and entering upon the journey of life without fortune or friends, unlearned in the lore of books, not even acquainted with the simple characters which make their silent pages speak the thoughts of others and reveal to the mind the rich treasures of human learning, he grappled with and overcame these obstacles to greatness with the same tireless energy and persistent courage which he brought to the accomplishment of every undertaking of his future life.

Endowed by nature with a manhood that knew no fear, an energy that knew no rest, a mind original and unique in its cast, which no system of ethics, no school of learning, could fetter or control, his character stands among the figures of American history without a model, grand and striking as the rugged mountains which girdle his beautiful Tennessee home.

In no country on earth, save in this land of free speech, free thought, and free institutions, could there have been such a career as ANDREW JOHNSON's. Making his first appearance as a legislator and representative of the people in the village council, and then as a delegate to the legislature of his State, he evinced at that early period the same inflexible integrity, stern devotion to duty, and strict adherence to the delegated powers of a public servant which governed him in his future political life.

Growing in public favor, and recognized by the people as the champion of their rights, the fearless defender of their interests, he was elected a member of the National Congress, and then, scarcely known, save by the sturdy yeomenry that dwelt among the mountains and in the green valleys of East Tennessee, he entered this hall and took his place among the counselors of the nation. Here he found a fitting field for the exercise of those wonderful powers with which nature had gifted him; here he entered an arena in which he could display all the prowess of the mighty athlete which he was soon to become.

Elected chief magistrate of his State, he filled the seat once held by a Sevier, a Carroll, and a Polk with an ability equal to his illustrious predecessors, and reflected renewed honor upon the great Commonwealth over which he presided.

Fortune still smiling upon her chosen favorite, he was elected by the legislature of Tennessee a Senator in the Congress of the nation, where he grappled in equal combat with the great orators and statesmen who then composed that august body.

Still moving onward in the fulfillment of the high destiny allotted him by nature, he was called by the voice of the people to the second highest office in their gift; and before its mantle had scarcely been adjusted, the providence of God placed in his hand the scepter wielded by the chief ruler of our great Republic.

This brief sketch of a single character, this short story, so plainly told, of a single life, covers events so strange and developments so startling, one might well suppose that the hand of the romancer had seized upon the pen of the historian and written upon a page swept by the wand of the magician. The unlettered youth, the country rustic, becoming by his own unaided exertions a polished orator, a learned legislator, a great leader of the people, and finally the ruler of his nation, presents a picture seldom drawn by the pen of the sober historian.

The name of ANDREW JOHNSON will go into history coupled with the great events which attracted the interest and attention of mankind during the age in which he lived.

Many of his public acts, as well as the general tenor of his life, endeared him in a peculiar manner to the hearts of the people, the humble masses of his countrymen. They followed and trusted him with a confidence and affectionrarely ever accorded before to an American politician, and in the strength of their devotion and exuberance of their enthusiasm they crowned him the people's sovereign.

Early in his public career there sprang into existence, as the offering and product of that restless spirit which has always pervaded American politics, ever seeking changes and innovations, a party organization teaching hostility to a large class of our people, and making the character of their religion and the place of their birth the test of political preferment. Gathering strength by the novelty of its teachings, and crossing the border of surrounding States, it was spreading over Tennessee like a rushing wave sweeping away all opposition, until it met in ANDREW JOHNSON a stern, relentless foe, under whose stalwart blows it was shattered to atoms, and it now only lives in the history of the past.

No marvel, then, that every man of foreign birth, who has found a home upon American soil, shelter and protection under the broad banner of our free Government, honors and reveres the name and memory of the enlightened statesman, the bold and generous champion who battled so gallantly to maintain for them the rights of American citizenship.

Identified with the people in all their feelings and sympathies, having an intuitive perception of their wants and interests, he was ever active in the furtherance of those measures of legislation peculiarly calculated for the protection of their rights and the advancement of their happiness.

While his unbending will and strong combative nature made him smite rudely and wrestle fiercely with rival leaders whom he encountered, sometimes bringing upon him the enmity of the great and the powerful, yet the weak and defenseless were always his friends.

Studying profoundly our theory of government, so congenial to his nature and instinctive convictions, he became one among the ablest expounders of that palladium of our liberties, the safeguard of our rights, the Constitution of our country. To this, as he construed it, he adhered with unyielding firmness during all his long official life; by this he was guided in all his public actions. That which fell short of its requirements or went beyond its limits received from him no mild rebuke, no gentle touch, but was the signal of instant combat.

Once fixed in his convictions, he followed them with an energy that never relaxed, an industry that never tired, a vigilance that never slept, and a courage that never faltered or deserted him.

In the great historical events which transpired during his busy, eventful life his nature rose to the dignity of the occasion, and in all the changing vicissitudes of his career he lost none of that fixedness of purpose and persistency of will which carried him over so many obstacles, from the obscurity of the village artisan to the world-wide fame of the great commoner.

Whether basking in the sunshine of popular favor as the idol of the hour or battling against the storm of party proscription, he remained steadfast in his faith of the final triumph of the principles for which he contended, the measures which he advocated.

When the folly and madness of the American people had culminated in a fierce storm of civil war; when millions of armed men rushed to battle; when our whole social and political structure reeled and trembled in the terrible convulsion, he had the firmness to resist the entreaties of his friends, the allurements of the highest ambition which their partiality could have gratified, and to pursue the convictions which led him in a different direction.

When, in the heat of partisan zeal, before the quiet dignity of the statesman and the calm reflection of the patriot had taken the place of the frenzied passions and vindictive enmities engendered by the war, he was arraigned for trial before hostile judges, charged with a violation of that instrument which he had made the study and guide of his life, here he appalled his accusers and won the plaudits of the world by a dignity and moral grandeur of deportment that might have saved Charles of England from the scaffold and a monarch of France from dying by the guillotine.

Firm and unbending before the fickle storm of public opinion, which was for the time beating against him, and making no effort to change its current, he retired from his high office with the dignity of a Roman senator and the unpretending patriotism of a Cincinnatus, and returned to the home in the mountains from which he had so often been called by the voice of the people.

He presented the spectacle—all too rare in modern history—of a man spending an entire life-time in his country's service, filling the highest station in its gift, holding in some measure both its purse and its sword, going back in the evening of his days to private life poorer than most of those who give only ordinary talents to the usual avocations of life.

No bribe ever found its way into his hand; no corruption ever stained his record; and it was the pride of his life, the boast of his friends, that even his enemies have borne willing testimony to the purity of his private and the honesty of his public life.

It is yet too soon to write impartially the history of this remarkable man. His combats are too recent; too many of the foemen with whom he contended are still living; the blows he dealt are yet too keenly felt. The snows of a single winter have not yet fallen upon his new-made grave in the village church-yard. In it let him rest until a future generation, unbiassed by the friendship or enmity of the present, shall sit in judgment upon his actions and accord him that place in history to which he shall be entitled.

The thoughts, feelings, and aspirations which have occupied great minds in life have sometimes been the burden of their last whisper as they were being forever enveloped in the gathering shadows of death.

When the great Napoleon lay dying in exile, long after his splendid career had closed, his mind wandered back to the days of his glory, when he was the leader of those invincible armies whose marches over Europe were lighted with the constant blaze of victory: he whispered with failing breath the same martial words which had rung over so many fields of battle.

When the great English admiral, the heroic Nelson, had fought his last fight, had won his last great victory, and was being borne bleeding, dying, from the bloody deck, he uttered those words which have gone into history and been inscribed beside his name high up upon the roll of naval heroes.

ANDREW JOHNSON, when about to step across the narrow stream which divides us from the broad ocean of eternity which spreads out beyond; when the sound of its rushing waters was falling upon his ear, unmindful of the terrors of the grim specter whose shadowy outline was drawing near, said to those around him: "Let my body be shrouded in the flag of the nation and my head be pillowed upon the Constitution of my country." What grander thought, what higher aspiration, could fill the mind of an American patriot and statesman in the hour of death!

No wonder, then, that those antagonisms growing out of party differences and bitter political strifes should have been softened or forever obliterated from the minds of his most relentless enemies, and that all over the civilized world men should feel that a great spirit had fallen when the lightning's flash, flying over valleys, along mountains, and under the billows of the ocean, brought the silent message, "ANDREW JOHNSON is dead!"

The aphorism that "republics are ungrateful" can no longer hold a place in truthful history. What king or potentate ever received higher honors from slaves and courtiers than the American people have conferred upon this untitled republican leader, making him the chief ruler of their nation while living, and, now that he is dead, the representatives of fifty millions of freemen pause in the business of legislation to do honor to his memory?

Every people, since the day the Romans planted their great empire upon the banks of the Tiber and the Greeks spread their civilization along the shores of the Mediterranean, have done honor to the fame and achievements of the great and illustrious of their countrymen after they were dead, whatever judgment they awarded them when living, and they have filled their galleries with paintings and studded their cities thick with monuments in commemoration of their deeds and in honor of their memory.

Nor have we been less generous to our illustrious dead than other and older nations of the world. The canvas upon which their features have been portrayed hangs from the pillars and decorates the walls of the Capitol, while their forms, cast in bronze or sculptured in marble, stand in the alcoves of the Rotunda like silent sentinels guarding the citadel of free institutions and American liberty. And though the glowing canvas may fade, the brass corrode, and the beautiful marble crumble into dust, yet their memory will live in story and song as long as tradition shall dwell in the human mind, and until the stream of human history shall be lost in the waveless sea of oblivion. Death has of a verity been hurling its shafts at shining marks, and taking its victims from the circle of the nation's great men.

Massachusetts has just buried Henry Wilson, her own great commoner, who, like his distinguished compeer, rose from the humblest origin to the highest stations and most distinguished honors, and the emblems of mourning that festoon this Hall and droop with the half-mast flag of our country attest the nation's sympathy with the ancient Commonwealth of the East.

In the performance of these ceremonies, it would be well if we would forever forget the differences, growing as well out of the providence of God as the folly of men, which have so long and so unhappily divided those whom the interest of civilization and the destiny of their race require to be brothers not only in political relations but in social feeling.

It were better if we could consecrate this hour to the service of the living as well as to the honor of the dead by burying in the graves of ANDREW JOHNSON and Henry Wilson the bitterness and hatreds which have so long burned in the hearts of our people. Let Massachusetts and Tennessee join hands over the tombs of their great statesmen and renew that broken bond of political union and fraternal affection which once bound them so nearly together.

Though they have entered the valley of the shadow of death, let us emerge from the shadow of our past misfortunes into the full brightness of that day the coming dawn of which already begins to gild with golden azure the heavy clouds which have so long hung upon our political horizon.

Now, in the opening of the centennial year of our national life, before the coming spring shall spread its vernal robe over the graves of our illustrious dead, let the yawning chasm rent by the throes of a horrid civil war be forever closed, and the blessings of prosperity, good government, and perpetual peace be vouchsafed to a people who have made themselves worthy to receive them.

ADDRESS OF MR. THROCKMORTON, OF TEXAS.

Mr. Speaker, being a native of Tennessee, and having had official relations with Mr. JOHNSON, I feel it to be a melancholy duty to join in seconding the resolutions now being considered. In doing so I desire to say Mr. JOHNSON, by what he was and by what he did, by his qualities, his fortunes, and his work, is entitled to prominent mention among the great leaders of his age and his country.

He is notably a representative of the common people of the land; of that class to whom the Republic must look for defense against foreign foes, upon whose broad shoulders the great industrial enterprises that minister so essentially to the necessities, comforts, and civilization of the nation rest; and who furnish the common sense from which the overruling sober second thought, so necessary to the preservation of our political equipoise, comes, and the sterling integrity that prompts all sacrifices and impels all great endeavors for patriotic purposes against either domestic or foreign foes. Without the advantages of wealth, social or influential aids; embarrassed by abject poverty; with the burdens of a dependent family, this child of the people, by sturdy toil, won his honorable success. He achieved competency, acquired knowledge, gained public notice and confidence; and from the humblest beginning arose step by step to the highest and most influential positions attainable by the most gifted and favored of the Republic, illustrating most fully in his career the beneficent and elevating effects of our free and liberal institutions. His success in life is not more noteworthy in the magnitude of difficulties surmounted and the honorable ends it compassed than by the simple and ordinary method by which it was accomplished. No magician preceded or accompanied him, by wand or lamp, to destroy his foes, build his palaces, or win his castles; but, living under institutions that furnished equal facilities for all, and gave equal motives to well-doing for each, under the movings of a great nature he recognized the dignity of labor and contemplated the victory as much and as certainly as the resultant thereof as does the farmer regard the harvest as the result of his toil. Not by trick, nor by fortune, nor by favor, nor by fortuitous circumstances, but by painstaking labor, he conquered competency, knowledge, public confidence, influence, position, and all the distinguishing qualities and successes that make up the record of his remarkable career; and he leaves as a legacy, not the least valuable of those bequeathed to his country in his example, that not only may the humblest citizen aspire to a career as honorable as that of ANDREW JOHNSON, but that none are so poor as not to possess the same homely appliances of success, the diligent use of which rendered him so distinguished.

He is a remarkable instance of that type of our great men who have been distinguished for the persistency with which they have adhered to their political convictions. Born in the State of North Carolina, and resident in Tennessee where the hero of New Orleans lived, and coming into public life when this great leader was prominent in the councils that governed the nation, his political views belonged to the school of that great man rather than to either those of Calhoun or Clay, antagonizing in some sort the extremes of each on the question then vexing the public mind relative to the supremacy of the State or national authority. He believed in the sanctity of the local governments, because guaranteed in their functions by the Constitution of the sisterhood of States; yet as to the political relations of the States to each other he recognized the Federal authority as supreme. When in 1861 his section embraced the Calhoun theory rather than the Jacksonian view, he remained steadfast to his convictions, notwithstanding the violent and overwhelming opposition of his section. When his party, while he was President, went to the other extreme, and so far pressed the national idea into legislation as to substantially destroy the constitutional rights and authority of the local governments, he refused to follow their leadership, and stood by his early convictions.

Again, he recognized in his early public life the supremacy of the civil authority over the military, as guaranteed by the Constitution. In later life, amid the distempers and passions bred by civil war, no partisan considerations, no persuasion of political friends, no provocation of political foes, could induce him to ignore or violate this cardinal principle of our institutions. Still another belief of his youth and of his mature years was one taught him when he was poor and friendless, and which he did not forget when he attained prosperity and distinction, that the people are not only the original depositaries of all power, under our form of government, but that they, in the exercise of the ballot and formation and influence of an intelligent and wholesome public opinion, are the conservators of free institutions. He was a man emphatically of the people, feeling that his personal citizenship exceeded in dignity any official position that he might hold; and he retained through life a profound confidence in the popular integrity and judgment. And when any great exigency was upon the country he looked not to cliques, nor to caucuses, nor to political conventions for relief or a wise solution of pending problems, but he always felt that, with free speech and a free press, the popular reference was the wisest, and always awaited the settlement by the people of the gravest questions with perfect confidence. He believed that not only the patriotism but the common sense of the people would be equal to any demand the country might make upon them, his consistency appearing not in uniform affiliation with any of the great parties, but in his persistent adherence to his convictions, despite party changes and party considerations.

Finally, ANDREW JOHNSON deserved well of the whole country, and especially so of the South; not only because a citizen and an efficient representative of the interests of that section in the highest councils of the nation, but particularly because of the policy pursued by him pending the existence of the trying ordeal to which that section was subjected in the process of political rehabilitation.

When the country, by the very crash of the conflict through which its unity and integrity were preserved, seemed to have been bewildered and cut loose from its moorings, and constitutional methods of restoration were deemed inadequate and were abandoned as insufficient, and peace and restoration were sought by proscription, he stood firm amid the general strife and wild confusion, imbued with the generous spirit and proposing to carry out the catholic and brave measures of his great and lamented predecessor. He, by counsel and message, by act and deed, while appreciating the fact that we were brethren separated from each other because of radically varying conceptions of the Constitution, honestly entertained, and not that either party was essentially vicious, or recreant to the traditions of the country or the memory of the fathers, perceived that political restoration brought privileges as broad as the duties that it imposed, and that no re-adjustment could be real that did not proceed on the basis of mutual respect, and did not conclude and culminate in mutual good-will; and that these great ends could only be attained and secured by constitutional methods. He abated nothing in his demand for obedience to law, yielded nothing of his love of country, but made, or endeavored to make, reconstruction as little humiliating to the defeated people of my section, and as little onerous, as the facts and necessities of the great occasion would permit.

A man of strong will, sometimes he seemed arbitrary; of positive convictions, he seemed dogmatic; of comprehensive views, looking not only at the beginning but to the end, he seemed impracticable; of profound convictions, and not swayed by considerations of expediency, he seemed unreasonable. With life's victory won by a struggle so sternly earnest that the nature developed by the very discipline that made it large and imposing became somewhat indurated, yet in simple manliness, sturdy integrity, and a personal fidelity to friend and country that never wavered, his was a grand character; and, take him all in all—his beginning, his work, and the end—he has not left his peer, and we shall scarcely in this generation look upon his like again.

His messages to Congress, in my judgment, rank among the ablest of American state papers, and will be regarded in the future as among the strongest vindications of the rights of the citizen and the States that have been produced by the statesmanship of our country.

When that auspicious day shall come, as I trust it will at no distant period, that the passions and prejudices engendered by the late sectional strife have been banished from the hearts of our people forever; when the American mind, North and South, East and West, can regard the prowess of the soldiery of both sections and the grand achievements of the military leaders on both sides and do justice alike to all, regardless of the cause or section represented, as representative types of American character and American greatness; when that time comes, and the popular heart is moved but by one impulse of devotion to the Union and the Constitution, then will the memory of Mr. JOHNSON live in the hearts of the masses of our countrymen, and then his faults, from which none are exempt, shall cease to be remembered.

The question being taken on the resolutions offered by Mr. McFARLAND, they were agreed to unanimously.

And accordingly (at four o'clock and thirty minutes p. m.) the House adjourned.

Printed in Dunstable, United Kingdom